8 STEPS TO SIDE CHARACTERS

HOW TO CRAFT SUPPORTING ROLES WITH
INTENTION, PURPOSE, AND POWER
WORKBOOK

SACHA BLACK

8 Steps to Side Characters: How to Craft Side Characters with Intention, Purpose, and Power Workbook

First Published July 2021, by Atlas Black Publishing

Edited by: Tim Seabrook, **Fifth Ring Press Proofing**
Cover design: Andrew Brown, **Design for Writers**

www.sachablack.co.uk

CONTENTS

Read Me First   1
Step 1 WTF is a Side Character?   3
Step 2 The Web of Connectivity and Theme   18
Step 3 Flesh and Blood   34
Step 4 Voice of an Angel   89
Step 5 What Do Side Characters Do Anyway?   138
Step 6 Arc Weaving   178
Step 7 Killing Your Darlings   208
Step 8 Fight to the Death   251
Want More?   293

Also by Sacha Black   295
About the Author   297

READ ME FIRST

I'm a stickler for all things practice. My son is learning to play the piano, he's a good little demon, I don't often have to demand he practices. For the most part, he knows if he wants to be able to play the Minecraft "Arch-Illager" theme song, he has to practice his scales and *Mary Had a Little Lamb* in order to build the muscle memory in his fingers and the skills in his brain to be able to play the harder stuff. So why aren't we writers the same way?

I know you're not like that, you're already reading a workbook filled with practice questions and examples for you to do intentional practice, but I like to stand on my soapbox for at least a paragraph.

One of the things I always quote in these workbook introductions is Malcom Gladwell. He's famed for saying it takes 10,000 hours of practice to master a skill. Except he's always misquoted. It's not just 10,000 hours, it's 10,000 *intentional* hours of practice. That means taking your weaknesses (or your strengths) and working on them intentionally. Doing exercises and muscular stretches that work different muscle areas and pushing them into fatigue so the muscle regenerates and grows stronger.

That is the purpose of this workbook for you. We're taking a specific muscle—our side character creation—and we're smashing the shit out of it in the writer's gym. Prepare thy musculature, it's going to be a ride, a whirl and a twirl. But by the end of it, you *will* have better, tighter, more depthy—that's totally a word, ahem—side characters.

Not to state the obvious, but this is a workbook. Which means, if you haven't read the companion textbook, I'd recommend you do. As this is a workbook, it deliberately assumes you've either read the full textbook or that you already understand the story building and character concepts in here. This workbook gives you the time and space to complete the exercises to help you craft the side characters your story needs. If you want the detail behind the book, then you'll need to read the *8 Steps to Side Characters: How to Craft Supporting Roles with Intention, Purpose and Power textbook* cover to cover. That said, I've tried to add enough information to each step that you can understand the concepts and complete the exercises.

I've tried to format the book to leave enough space for you to answer some of the shorter questions inside this book—for those reading the paperback, anyway. Where you're required to write full scenes, longer answers or undertake explorative exercises you'll need additional paper. Last, in the vast majority of cases, I've asked questions in references to your "five" main side characters. If you have less, that's fine, if you have more, also fine but you'll need additional paper.

Still with me? Then welcome on board.

Let's shake up our side characters and shimmy on down.

STEP 1 WTF IS A SIDE CHARACTER?

Regardless of "what" your story is about, it's *always* about change. All stories, regardless of genre, tropes and characters are about change. Your protagonist is the biggest embodiment of this change, but all characters are the embodiment of some aspect of that change or idea inside your story.

Characters draw the idea into reality. They are a metaphor that makes the idea and concept real to us. Characters show us through the detail of their actions, their emotions and interactions what the idea really means.

Side characters specifically then, are the arteries in a protagonist-heart, they are new perspectives and viewpoints, conflict generators and subplot fulfillers. When you get to the heart of a story and its characters, all characters are the embodiment of the idea behind your story. In other words, your theme.

Characters manage this by drawing theme into reality through engaging in conversation, action and obstacles all based on that theme. Characters are a metaphor that make the idea and concept of theme real to us. It is through the detail of character actions, emotions and interactions that we come to understand what theme really means.

Look at this like this, if your book and theme were a math equation, the protagonist would be the solution. The antagonist would be the wrong answer and your side characters would be the working out and alternative solutions you discarded along the way.

The three types of side character are: major, minor and cameos.

Cameo Characters

Cameos are the briefest stars. They play a very short, succinct role, such as a throwaway perfunctory line, opening a door for the protagonist, a throng of faceless beings in a crowd, etc.

Think Stan Lee, the Marvel comic author. Stan, may he Rest In Peace, starred in every Marvel movie ever made. He was only in shot for a few brief seconds and then he was gone. In *The Trial of the Incredible Hulk*, he played the role of a jury foreman. In *Thor*, Stan tries to pull the hammer using his truck. In *Captain America: The First Avenger*, he plays an elderly general.

My favorite example of a cameo is the woman in the red dress from *The Matrix* movie. Neo—the protagonist—is in a simulator, he's walking through the world, the location looks very much like a regular downtown New York street. Busy, and bustling with people. Morpheus (his mentor) is walking slightly ahead of him telling him important information. Everyone in the simulation is in bland black suits, and professional clothes. Everyone looks the same. Morpheus asks whether he's paying attention. He was, until a woman in a red dress walked past him. The only human wearing even a hint of color. So of course, his attention is taken away from Morpheus, who asks him to look back at the woman. When he does, the woman is gone and an enemy agent is holding a gun to Neo's face. The point in the film is that anyone can be an agent. The point it makes about cameos is that they appear one second and are gone the next. Oh, and the only thing you remember in the *Matrix*—if at all—is that there was some rather attractive lady wearing a bright red dress.

How much detail do you add for cameos? Well, you can describe their appearance if you want, but cameos aren't around long enough for your reader to remember much about them and frankly, they don't need to. So why fill their brain with useless shit? Stick to giving them the good stuff.

Cameos don't need subplots or character arcs either. They don't even need a name. Most of the time, the author creates some kind of label for the character. Like the aforementioned "woman in the red dress" or perhaps the barman or the girl with the teddy.

Minor Characters

Minor side characters are a little bit more enduring than cameos. While they appear on page a few more times than a cameo, they are still just an extra in a film. Minor character roles include bringing information, performing a repetitive role like a barman or receptionist in a location the protagonist frequents on more than one occasion.

These guys appear, do their dirty business and leave again.

While their role may be important to the "world", the magic system, the legal system or even the plot, it has no sway over the protagonist or his story arc, save for transactional exchanges. The exception to this is a minor character who brings information that changes what a protagonist does.

Examples of minor characters include Mr. Filch (the janitor) from the *Harry Potter* series, Wheezy from *Toy Story 2*, Tiny Tim from *A Christmas Carol*, Magda from *The Hunger Games*, Kit Fisto from *Star Wars*, Zed from *Pulp Fiction*.

You should probably describe a minor character and ensure they have some kind of defining characteristic that makes them recognizable enough they're at least a smidge memorable. After all, your hero and your reader will encounter them more than once.

Minor characters don't need subplots or character arcs either because they only need to create the illusion of "real" character.

Major Side Characters

Major side characters are one step removed from the protagonist.

The headlines. Major characters…

- are three dimensional characters which means they need depth
- may have a point of view or narrate parts in the story
- likely have subplots dedicated to them
- likely have arcs
- are usually scarce in numbers, perhaps two to five of them
- represent one angle of the theme

This means they have a meaningful role to play in the story. They shape and sway the protagonist as well as creating conflict and plot problems and equally help to solve them just as frequently. Perhaps your major character is the catalyst that helps the hero to change or maybe they're one of the obstacles preventing them from changing. Major characters should also be connected to the theme of your story. While the protagonist represents the answer to the story question, your major side characters will likely be some variation on the theme too.

Character Quantity

The quantity of each type of side character you have is entirely dependent on the type of story you tell. Broadly speaking for the average story, it's likely you'll have more cameos than any other type of character. You'll have fewer minor characters than cameo, but still a good chunk of them. But you'll only have a handful of major characters because of the page time they require to fulfill their role and create sufficient depth.

Identify five cameo characters from either your favorite books (preferably from the genre you write) or TV shows and movies.

1.

2.

3.

4.

5.

Identify five minor characters from either your favorite books (preferably from the genre you write) or TV shows and movies.

1.

2.

3.

4.

5.

Identify five major characters from either your favorite books (preferably from the genre you write) or TV shows and movies.

1.

2.

3.

4.

5.

Pick one of the cameos mentioned above, what description is used for them? Note down all the information you know about that character.

·

·

·

·

·

·

Pick one of the minor characters mentioned above, what description is used for them? Note down all the information you know about that character.

·

·

·

·

·

·

Pick one of the major characters mentioned above, what description is used for them? Note down all the information you know about that character.

·

·

.

.

.

.

Reflecting on the last three questions, can you see the difference in volume of information you know as a reader about each of these types of character?

.

.

.

.

.

.

Thinking about your story now, what is the main "change" in your novel that your protagonist goes through?

.

.

.

.

.

.

Describe your protagonist's starting status and how that's different from their status at the end of your book.

.

.

.

.

.

.

How does your protagonist embody your theme?

.

.

.

.

.

.

Note down your main major side characters:

1.

2.

3.

4.

5.

Now looking at those main side characters. How does each one represent the theme in your novel in a way that's different to the protagonist?

.

.

.

.

.

.

Note down your main minor side characters:

1.

2.

3.

4.

5.

6.

7.

8.

9.

10.

Note down any cameo side characters you know of:

1.

2.

3.

4.

5.

6.

7.

8.

9.

10.

Character versus Characterization

A short, but no less important clarification. Character and characterization are often used interchangeably, hell, even I do it. But I probably shouldn't because while they sound the same, and while they're part and parcel of a whole, they are not, in fact, the same thing. Clarity is my drug of choice, thus, let us ensure we are crystal about the two:

Character is:

internal. It's the *who* of who a character is, the traits and whatever is at their core. Character is what you don't see, it's subtext and shadows, it's the foundations and pillars laid in a house—you know they're there supporting the house, you just can't see them.

Characterization is:

everything on the surface. It's the physical appearance of your character. It's the clothes they wear, the tone of their dialogue, the observable actions in a story. Characterization is the embodiment of character in a scene. It's what the reader sees and what shows them the "character" they can't see. Characterization and character effect and influence each other, they are osmotic in nature, they percolate between, through and around each other.

Character is focused inward. Characterization, is mostly focused outward toward the reader. They are the yin and yang of characters.

Note: both character and characterization should be shown and not told, it is far more revealing and engaging for a reader to be shown than told these aspects.

Focusing on your major side characters, note down the following:

Side Character 1

Describe their character:

.

.

-

-

-

-

Now note down three things you will use to show their character through characterization:

1.

2.

3.

Side Character 2

Describe their character:

-

-

-

-

-

-

Now note down three things you will use to show their character through characterization:

1.

2.

3.

Side Character 3

Describe their character:

.

.

.

.

.

.

    Now note down three things you will use to show their character through characterization:

1.

2.

3.

Side Character 4

Describe their character:

.

-

-

-

-

-

Now note down three things you will use to show their character through characterization:

1.

2.

3.

Side Character 5

Describe their character:

-

-

-

-

-

-

Now note down three things you will use to show their character through characterization:

1.

2.

3.

STEP 2 THE WEB OF CONNECTIVITY AND THEME

Theme is the what of what your story is about. If your book were a body and the plot was its skin, the theme would be what's underneath the skin. A simple way to look at this is that the theme is an exploration of the question your book poses, and the moral lesson is the answer the characters find and learn. Ultimately, theme tends to be some exploration of the universal human condition like love, good vs evil or sacrifice.

The web of connectivity is the concept that each element of a book is threaded together like the threads in a spider's web. Each part of a novel—the characters, theme, twists, arcs, and subplots—are all seamlessly woven together. I liken the concentric circle in a web to those big plots, theme and twists, etc. and the major structural threads connecting to walls and branches and leaves as support, are your side characters.

To come up with theme, study your characters, plot and subplots. What aspects of it are universal to all humans? Examine the choice your hero is making in the climax of your novel. Or, decide the message you'd like your readers to go away with. You could also start with your story hook and see if you can work out what question connects to it.

Characters can represent your book's theme in a variety of ways:

- A positive representation of the theme
- A negative representation of the theme
- A flip flop arc from a negative to positive representation of the theme
- A flip flop arc from positive to negative representation of the theme

In any book, you usually have a character representing the theme in each of the following ways:

- A character who always sticks to the theme truth or theme message
- A character who always sticks to a theme lie i.e. in the above example, love is not enough
- A character who moves from believing a truth about the theme to believing a lie
- A character who moves from believing a lie about the theme to believing a truth

Let's look at this in practice, the below is a worked example from the book I'm currently writing, *The Scent of Death:*

Mallory Mortimer, the protagonist, wants to save everyone he loves. The one word theme is "saving" the theme sentence is something along the lines of: *if you love someone, you should save them.* This is what Mallory embodies. But let's look at how I've represented variations of that theme with the other characters.

- Frank [surname pending] is gay and in the closet and struggling to come out in order to save himself. *Theme representation—A character who moves from believing a lie about the theme to believing a truth.*
- Pearl Rafferty [the love interest] is strong and independent and doesn't want saving because she can do

it herself thank you very much. *Theme representation—A character who always sticks to a theme lie i.e. Pearl doesn't need saving.*

- Pearl's mum wants to save kids by fostering them. *Theme representation—A character who always sticks to the theme truth or theme message—Pearl's mum will stop at nothing to save the kids.*

- Pearl's father works for an environmental charity and is trying to save the Earth. *Theme representation—much like his wife, Pearl's father is saving the planet instead of kids and thus is a character who always sticks to the theme truth or theme message.*

- Mal's mother is an alcoholic and can't save herself unless she chooses to. *Theme representation—like Mal, his mother is a character who moves from believing a lie about the theme to believing a truth. Mal's mother didn't believe she was worthy of saving no matter who she loved or who loved her.*

- Mal's father has a terminal illness, he wants to save his soul by asking for forgiveness. *Theme representation—this is a tricky one because Mal's father is a poking rod I'm using to make Mal question his morals. On the outside, Mal's father is a very negative character, but in the story, he's actually a character who always sticks to the theme truth or theme message, as no matter his past or his past relationships, he's trying to save both Mal and himself.*

Every single character is a twist on the theme. All of them are trying to save something, whether that's saving themselves, the environment, children, or actively trying to not be saved.

To give your characters meaning, ensure their subplots are forcing them to answer a thematic question that's a variation of the protagonist's. Now it's over to you. Let's connect your side characters to your book's theme.

∾

Thinking about your five favorite books (or TV shows and movies) from the genre you write, note down the theme for each below:

1.

2.

3.

4.

5.

What is your theme in one-word?

.

.

What is your theme in one sentence?

.

.

.

.

Now expand and explore your theme in a paragraph.

.

.

.

.

.

.

.

.

What is your story hook?

.

.

.

.

What is the moral or thematic question your protagonist will answer?

.

.

.

.

What aspects of your plot, side characters and story represent the human condition?

.

.

·

·

What message or feeling would you like readers to go away with?

·

·

·

·

Brainstorm 10 different ways you could explore your book theme, if you don't have one, use the theme "trust".

1.

2.

3.

4.

5.

6.

7.

8.

9.

10.

How do your major side characters embody the theme?

1.

2.

3.

4.

5.

Which character or characters are a positive representation of the theme?

.

.

.

.

How do they positively represent the theme?

.

.

.

.

Write a short scene showing this flip flop using your own novel.

If you don't have a story you're currently working on, use the theme "trust".

-
-
-
-
-
-
-
-
-
-
-

Which character or characters are a negative representation of the theme?

-
-
-

.

How do they negatively represent the theme?

.

.

.

.

Write a short scene showing this flip flop using your own novel. If you don't have a story you're currently working on, use the theme "trust".

.

.

.

.

.

.

.

.

.

.

.

.

Which character or characters flip flop from a negative to positive representation of the theme?

.

.

.

.

How do they flip flop their representation of the theme?

.

.

.

.

Write a short scene showing this flip flop using your own novel. If you don't have a story you're currently working on, use the theme "trust".

.

.

.

.

·

·

·

·

·

·

·

·

Which character or characters flip flop from a positive to negative representation of the theme?

·

·

·

·

How do they flip flop their representation of the theme?

·

·

·

·

Write a short scene showing this flip flop using your own novel. If you don't have a story you're currently working on, use the theme "trust".

·

·

·

·

·

·

·

·

·

·

·

Which character sticks to the theme truth or theme message throughout your novel?

·

·

·

.

Write a short scene showing this rigid sticking to the theme truth despite pressure from other characters. Use your own novel theme. If you don't have a story you're currently working on, use the theme "trust".

.

.

.

.

.

.

.

.

.

.

.

Which character sticks to a theme lie throughout your novel?

.

.

.

.

Write a short scene showing this rigid sticking to the theme lie despite pressure from other characters. Use your own novel theme. If you don't have a story you're currently working on, use the theme "trust".

.

.

.

.

.

.

.

.

.

.

Which character moves from believing a truth about the theme to believing a lie?

.

.

.

.

Write a short scene showing this flip flop using your own novel. If you don't have a story you're currently working on, use the theme "trust".

.

.

.

.

.

.

.

.

.

.

Which character moves from believing a lie about the theme to believing a truth?

.

.

.

.

Write a short scene showing this flip flop using your own novel. If you don't have a story you're currently working on, use the theme "trust".

.

.

.

.

.

.

.

.

.

.

.

STEP 3 FLESH AND BLOOD

Fleshing out side characters can be a tricky job when they're not allowed to dominate the page. But you have some tools in your author tool bag, the most dominant of which include a character's actions and their dialogue. Let's dive into making your side characters all fleshy and plump.

Side Character Whys

Side characters exist as a story function, they either support or hinder the protagonist among other things. Although we all know that's what they were created for, you still need to create the *illusion* of a "full" character with depth and all the trimmings a protagonist would have without giving them the time or page space to actually display it all. One of the ways of creating this illusion is to ensure your character has more than one "why".

In fact, side characters need three different types of "why" throughout your story:

- A protagonist why—in other words are they supporting or hindering the protagonist and why? Is it because

they're a best friend? Do they disagree with the
protagonists values? etc.

- A life why—in order to make your side character seem
  "real" they need a reason for existing outside of the
  protagonist. What is *their* goal? What do they want in
  life? Are they trying to come out to their family? Are they
  trying to get onto the swim team? Get a new job etc.
- A scene why—too often side characters appear in a
  scene with no reason for being there. They hang around
  the scene, don't do much or say much, don't impact the
  story, tension or conflict, and then the scene ends. Erm,
  no. If a character is in a scene, they need a reason why
  they're there. What are they doing?

Studying your five major side characters, explore their protagonist and life why.

Side Character 1 Protagonist Why:

.

.

.

.

.

Side Character 1 Life Why:

.

.

.

.

.

Side Character 2 Protagonist Why:

.

.

.

.

.

Side Character 2 Life Why:

.

.

.

.

Side Character 3 Protagonist Why:

.

.

.

-

-

Side Character 3 Life Why:

-

-

-

-

-

Side Character 4 Protagonist Why:

-

-

-

-

-

Side Character 4 Life Why:

-

-

-

.

.

Side Character 5 Protagonist Why:

.

.

.

.

.

Side Character 5 Life Why:

.

.

.

.

.

Base Emotions

One of my dear writing friends wears a tattoo equation quote from Jack Canfield on her arm. It says this:

$$E + R = O$$

Event plus reaction equals emotion. Canfield argues that every outcome you experience is actually the summed conclusion of whatever the event was and your reaction to it. Which makes complete sense in fiction as well as reality. This means your side characters need emotions, and they need to use those emotions when they react to the events in your story.

Everyone has a baseline emotion. Take me for example, I'm a conniption—always in a state of hyper excitement or hyper rage. Of course, I moderate that depending on the situation, but those are my prevailing emotions.

In fiction, if you had a character with those two emotions, they would still moderate for different situations. For example, if you had two characters in a sad situation, one might cry, but another character might get angry-sad instead of tearful. They're still sad, they're just sad presented differently.

For your five major side characters, what is their base emotion/s? (Don't pick more than two and try to stick with one).

Side Character 1:

.

.

Side Character 2: .

.

.

Side Character 3:

.

.

Side Character 4:

.

.

Side Character 5:

.

.

Keeping that emotion in mind, how does that baseline emotion change and manifest when they experience the following:

A stressful event:

Side Character 1:

.

.

Side Character 2:

.

.

Side Character 3:

.

.

Side Character 4:

.

.

Side Character 5:

.

.

A happy event:
Side Character 1:

.

.

Side Character 2:

.

.

Side Character 3:

.

.

Side Character 4:

.

.

Side Character 5:

.

.

A sad event:
Side Character 1:

.

.

Side Character 2:

.

.

Side Character 3:

.

.

Side Character 4:

.

.

Side Character 5:

.

.

An event that makes them angry:
Side Character 1:

.

.

Side Character 2:

.

.

Side Character 3:

.

.

Side Character 4:

.

.

Side Character 5:

.

.

Side Character Introductions

When your side character first enters the story, you need to introduce them. But that doesn't mean you have to focus only on their physicality. The physical description is important or your readers hop off and create character appearances on their own which leads to a jarring effect when you finally do describe a character. But it's not always the most important aspect of an entrance. You need to decide what the priority is with a character's introduction. Is it how they look? Is it how they make the protagonist feel?

Or perhaps how they make another character feel? Is it a single trait you want to be salient? Or is it something else entirely?

Is there a part of their physical appearance that you *need* the reader to know about? Is there a part of their physical personality that tells the reader about their psychological personality or something about their inner core? Then that's the priority for an introductory description.

Pick one or two salient elements for your character description and make them stand out and have meaning to the story. It's important to remember that every time we meet your side character, their specific distinguishing feature is described differently. If your guy has blue eyes the first time we meet him, how about having his eyes show his emotion the second time, or match the atmosphere, or changed in some way rather than highlighting the same "blue" color again.

Let's look at your five main side characters.

Side Character 1:

What feeling do you want to leave the reader or protagonist with after meeting them?

.

.

.

.

What aspect of their physical appearance *shows* the reader the most about their personality?

.

.

.

What is their standout feature?

Write a one paragraph introduction for your character:

Now, write two new paragraphs, one for the character's second and third entrances. Make sure you approach their physicality in a different way, examining and deepening your descriptions each time.

Entrance 2:

.

.

.

.

.

.

.

.

Entrance 3:

.

.

.

.

.

.

.

Side Character 2:

What feeling do you want to leave the reader or protagonist with after meeting them?

·

·

·

·

What aspect of their physical appearance *shows* the reader the most about their personality?

·

·

·

·

What is their standout feature?

·

·

·

·

Write a one paragraph introduction for your character:

·

·

·

·

·

·

·

·

Now, write two new paragraphs, one for the character's second and third entrances. Make sure you approach their physicality in a different way, examining and deepening your descriptions each time.

Entrance 2:

·

·

·

·

·

·

·

·

Entrance 3:

-
-
-
-
-
-
-
-

Side Character 3:

What feeling do you want to leave the reader or protagonist with after meeting them?

-
-
-
-

What aspect of their physical appearance *shows* the reader the most about their personality?

-

.

.

.

What is their standout feature?

.

.

.

.

Write a one paragraph introduction for your character:

.

.

.

.

.

.

.

Now, write two new paragraphs, one for the character's second and third entrances. Make sure you approach their physicality in a different way, examining and deepening your descriptions each time.

Entrance 2:

-

-

-

-

Entrance 3:

-

-

-

-

Side Character 4:

What feeling do you want to leave the reader or protagonist with after meeting them?

-

-

-

-

What aspect of their physical appearance *shows* the reader the most about their personality?

-

-

-

-

What is their standout feature?

-

-

-

-

Write a one paragraph introduction for your character:

-

-

-

-

-

-

-

Now, write two new paragraphs, one for the character's second and third entrances. Make sure you approach their physicality in a different way, examining and deepening your descriptions each time.

Entrance 2:

.

.

.

.

Entrance 3:

.

.

.

.

Side Character 5:

What feeling do you want to leave the reader or protagonist with after meeting them?

.

.

.

.

What aspect of their physical appearance *shows* the reader the most about their personality?

-
-
-
-

What is their standout feature?

-
-
-
-

Write a one paragraph introduction for your character:

-
-
-
-
-
-

Now, write two new paragraphs, one for the character's second and third entrances. Make sure you approach their physicality in a different way, examining and deepening your descriptions each time.

Entrance 2:

Entrance 3:

Perfectly Flawed

Having perfect characters is a cardinal sin, make sure your side characters have flaws because it makes them more relatable. Alongside banishing perfect characters you need to banish the "must be likable" myth. I'm going to say this once but with force:

Characters don't need to be likable they need to be interesting.

But of course, unlikable still needs to be appealing or your readers switch off. To make the unlikable appealing, you can:

- Give them at least one positive trait
- Create a relatable wound
- Give them a moral line they won't cross
- Give them an expertise in something
- Have them demonstrate duty or kindness towards others
- Have the capacity to change—even if they don't actually change, having the capacity is more important than changing

For your side characters who are unlikeable, use the space below to explore how you will make them appealing using the bullets above.

Unlikable Side Character 1—how will you make them appealing?

.

.

.

.

Explore their capacity to change, will they or won't they? How *could* they change even if they don't actually end up changing?

.

.

.

.

Unlikable Side Character 2—how will you make them appealing?

.

.

.

.

Explore their capacity to change, will they or won't they? How *could* they change even if they don't actually end up changing?

.

.

.

.

Unlikable Side Character 3—how will you make them appealing?

.

.

.

.

Explore their capacity to change, will they or won't they? How *could* they change even if they don't actually end up changing?

.

.

.

.

Origin Stories

Your major side characters are likely to need origin stories. What is an origin story? An origin story simply explains how a character came to be that character. The importance of an origin story for a side character is to explain what fundamental parts of their history has shaped them into the character they are today. You need to include whatever wound or flaw is most salient for that character.

There are a three purposes for having an origin story and if you're not hitting all or at least some of them then your character probably doesn't need one.

- Purpose 1: to show why your character needs to change (i.e. if they have an arc they may need an origin story)
- Purpose 2: explain the traits they're displaying in your current story (i.e. the consequence of their wound)
- Purpose 3: to create consequences

Purposes aside, there are some common mistakes you should avoid with origin stories:

1. Giving too much page time to a side character origin story.
2. Making the origin story about the character's past instead of the present in the current story. Origin stories should have relevance and an impact on the present story.

3. Opening your book with the origin story or dropping it
   in too early on.

So keeping those mistakes and the reasons for having an origin
story in mind, let's dig into our five main side character's back-
grounds.

Side Character 1:

What were the most significant events in your characters past?

.

.

.

.

Are there any painful or overly happy memories?

.

.

.

.

Who or what influenced the character?

.

.

.

.

What kind of home or background does your character come from?

-
-
-
-

If you had to pick one emotion to summarize the character's childhood, what would it be?

-
-
-
-

Why is their origin story relevant to your current plot?

-
-
-
-

Write your side character's origin story in the space below:

-

.

.

.

.

.

.

.

.

.

.

.

.

.

.

Side Character 2:
What were the most significant events in your characters past?

.

.

.

.

Are there any painful or overly happy memories?

.

.

.

.

Who or what influenced the character?

.

.

.

.

What kind of home or background does your character come from?

.

.

.

.

If you had to pick one emotion to summarize the character's

childhood, what would it be?

-
-
-
-

Why is their origin story relevant to your current plot?

-
-
-
-

Write your side character's origin story in the space below:

-
-
-
-
-
-

.

.

.

.

.

.

.

.

Side Character 3:
What were the most significant events in your characters past?

.

.

.

.

Are there any painful or overly happy memories?

.

.

.

.

Who or what influenced the character?

.

.

.

.

What kind of home or background does your character come from?

.

.

.

.

If you had to pick one emotion to summarize the character's childhood, what would it be?

.

.

.

.

Why is their origin story relevant to your current plot?

.

.

.

.

Write your side character's origin story in the space below:

.

.

.

.

.

.

.

.

.

.

.

.

.

.

.

Side Character 4:
What were the most significant events in your characters past?

.

.

.

.

Are there any painful or overly happy memories?

.

.

.

.

Who or what influenced the character?

.

.

.

.

What kind of home or background does your character come from?

·

·

·

·

If you had to pick one emotion to summarize the character's childhood, what would it be?

·

·

·

·

Why is their origin story relevant to your current plot?

·

·

·

·

Write your side character's origin story in the space below:

·

-
-
-
-
-
-
-
-
-
-
-
-
-
-

Side Character 5:
What were the most significant events in your characters past?

-
-

.

.

Are there any painful or overly happy memories?

.

.

.

.

Who or what influenced the character?

.

.

.

.

What kind of home or background does your character come from?

.

.

.

.

If you had to pick one emotion to summarize the character's

childhood, what would it be?

.

.

.

.

Why is their origin story relevant to your current plot?

.

.

.

.

Write your side character's origin story in the space below:

.

.

.

.

.

.

.

.

.

.

.

.

.

.

.

.

Flashbacks

There are a number of reasons for and against using flashbacks. Like the fact that by definition the action in the flashback is already over because it happened in the past. Thus you're pulling the reader out of the story and the present time. But equally, a flashback can show the reader an aspect of character they haven't seen.

A flashback needs to serve a purpose like:

- Driving the plot forward by motivating, inspiring or demotivating the protagonist
- Reveal information or a secret that helps or hinders the protagonist
- Deepen characterization of either the protagonist or the side character
- Deepen the emotional connection with the reader

One easy way to create flashbacks is to use a trigger to help you get into and back out of the flashback. Triggers include "old" banter, a photograph or object, a newspaper article—anything that jogs the memory. For example:

> I walked into the room as Sandy handed a key to Brandon. Iron rust flaked off the stem and floated to the floor **[entry trigger]** I knew that key.
>
> The last time she gave Brandon that key was the day Danny died. She'd handed it over, smooth and shiny with newness, and all three of us went to the barn to finish Danny's new cot. We'd sanded and nailed the wooden crib for hours. Every rivet and bar was perfect. As the sun set, a breeze rippled through the barn door, dragging dust balls, dead leaves and plant detritus inside. A shriek, hollow and sharp tore, through the air. My skin crawled. Brandon froze. It was the kind of cry that cut scars into your memories.
>
> I glanced at the Key in Brandon's hand, **[exit trigger]** an antique now, but the screams were just as fresh.

Brainstorm a list of 10 triggers you could use in your own story, think about items that are important to your characters or perhaps their backstory.

1.

2.

3.

4.

5.

6.

7.

8.

9.

10.

In the space below, choose one of your side characters and think of a flashback that includes them.

Side Character 1:

Using the list of potential purposes above, identify the purpose of the flashback for this character.

.

.

.

.

What trigger are you using or how will you get into and out of the flashback seamlessly?

.

.

.

.

Write the flashback in the space below:

.

.

-
-
-
-
-
-
-
-
-
-
-
-

Side Character 2:

Using another side character, create a new flashback for them. Using the list of potential purposes above, identify the purpose of the flashback for this character.

-
-

.

.

What trigger are you using or how will you get into and out of the flashback seamlessly?

.

.

.

.

Write the flashback in the space below:

.

.

.

.

.

.

.

.

.

.

·

·

·

·

·

·

Humor

So many authors are afraid of using humor. But there are a ton of different types of humor you can use to create new flavor to your story and characters.

For example: sarcasm, dry humor, puns, cliches, innuendos, self-depreciation, toilet humor, dark humor, Monty Python style humor, and slapstick to name a few.

If you're really not comfortable including humor, then perhaps plump for sharpness.

Thinking about your five favorite books (or TV shows and movies) from the genre you write, note down the type of humor the funniest character has from each story:

1.

2.

3.

4.

5.

What are your character's sense of humors like?
Protagonist:

·

·

·

Side Character 1:

·

·

·

Side Character 2:

·

·

·

Side Character 3:

·

·

·

Side Character 4:

·

.

.

Side Character 5:

.

.

.

Anchoring Characters

If you have a large cast of characters, then anchoring some of them makes it easier for your readers to remember who they are. Anchors are literally objects, words, locations or emotions that are associated with a particular character. For example, a character could be a barman and thus is seen almost exclusively inside the bar.

Thinking about your five favorite books (or TV shows and movies) from the genre you write, note down how a character is anchored in each story:

1.

2.

3.

4.

5.

What anchors do your side characters have, if any?
Side Character 1:

-

-

-

Side Character 2:

-

-

-

Side Character 3:

-

-

-

Side Character 4:

-

-

-

Side Character 5:

-

-

Side Character Relationships

While the protagonist is the core in your story, they're going to have relationships; be they positive, negative or axe-to-the-face with the other characters in your story. It's important your protagonist (and side characters) relate to each other in different ways. Their relationships shouldn't be clones. I'm sure you behave differently with your mate from your martial arts club than you do with the parents at your kid's school.

Thinking about your five favorite books (or TV shows and movies) from the genre you write, note down the type of relationship the protagonist has with two separate side characters:

Story 1 is:

Relationship with character A:

Relationship with character B:

How does the author show the differences in those relationships?

-

-

-

Story 2 is:

-

-

Relationship with character A:

-

-

-

Relationship with character B:

-

-

-

How does the author show the differences in those relationships?

-

-

Story 3 is:

Relationship with character A:

Relationship with character B:

How does the author show the differences in those relationships?

Story 4 is:

·

Relationship with character A:

·

·

·

Relationship with character B:

·

·

·

How does the author show the differences in those relationships?

·

·

·

Story 5 is:

·

·

Relationship with character A:

·

.

.

Relationship with character B:

.

.

.

How does the author show the differences in those relationships?

.

.

.

Thinking about your five main side characters, describe their relationships with the protagonist and two other characters. Are there any quirks or identifiable behaviors in their relationships? What is the tone of their relationship and how do they communicate?

Side Character 1—relationship with protagonist:

.

.

.

Relationship with character A:

.

.

.

Relationship with character B:

.

.

.

Side Character 2—relationship with protagonist:

.

.

.

Relationship with character A:

.

.

.

Relationship with character B:

.

.

.

Side Character 3—relationship with protagonist:

.

.

.

Relationship with character A:

.

.

.

Relationship with character B:

.

.

.

Side Character 4—relationship with protagonist:

.

.

.

Relationship with character A:

.

-

-

Relationship with character B:

-

-

-

Side Character 5—relationship with protagonist:

-

-

-

Relationship with character A:

-

-

-

Relationship with character B:

-

-

-

STEP 4 VOICE OF AN ANGEL

Author voice is changeable. An author's voice is simply the culmination of all aspects of their craft and prose choices. For example the sound of their voice will include things like:

- Your choice of verbs and adjectives
- The pattern of your punctuation and grammar (one author might choose to use Oxford commas, another might refuse)
- Use or not of adverbs
- Length of sentences
- The balance of dialogue to prose
- Accented dialogue or not
- The quantity of descriptive prose
- The style of your prose, is it full of metaphors or do you use a cleaner style of description?
- The size of your cast of characters
- POV

Thinking about your five favorite books from the genre you write, note down a description for the author's voice.

1.

2.

3.

4.

5.

Describe your voice or the voice you're trying to emulate in a few words below:

.

.

.

.

Character voice is not changeable. Their voice is *who* they are. If they're a nerdy astrophysicist who always uses ridiculously big words, they're still going to be an astrophysicist who uses ridiculously big words at the end of the story no matter how they've grown and changed as a person in the story. So contrast your above paragraph with your five main side characters. Describe the voices you're trying to create for them:

Side Character 1:

.

.

.

.

How is this different to your author voice?

.

.

.

.

Side Character 2:

.

.

.

.

How is this different to your author voice?

.

.

.

.

Side Character 3:

.

-

-

-

How is this different to your author voice?

-

-

-

-

Side Character 4:

-

-

-

-

How is this different to your author voice?

-

-

-

-

Side Character 5:

.

.

.

.

How is this different to your author voice?

.

.

.

.

One exercise I particularly like, is to allow the character to tell you their backstory in their voice. Imagine they're talking to you, telling you their origin story or how they came to be in the location your story is set. How would *they* tell you the story? Do they flounder and talk in circles? Are they cheap with their words and use little description or detail? Do they have an accent?

Allowing a character to tell you their backstory in their own voice not only helps you shape the character's voice, it also helps you create their backstory.

Use the space below to interview your side characters and get them to tell you about their past in their own voice.

Side Character 1:

.

.

-

-

-

-

-

-

-

-

-

-

-

-

-

Side Character 2:

-

-

-
-
-
-
-
-
-
-
-
-
-
-
-

Side Character 3:

-
-
-

-

-

-

-

-

-

-

-

-

-

-

Side Character 4:

-

-

-

-

-

-

-

-

-

-

-

-

-

-

-

Side Character 5:

-

-

-

-

-

-

-

-

-

-

-

-

-

-

-

-

Now, looking back at the five different voices. Use the space below to reflect on each character and the main differences between their voices:

-

-

-

-

Reflecting on your paragraphs above, what elements of your sentences make the character voice the strongest?

.

.

.

.

.

.

The Character Lens

In previous books, I've discussed the concept of a hero lens, which is:

"Everything the hero does, sees, feels and thinks, encloses your reader into a tiny literary lens. Nothing happens in your book unless your protagonist experiences it. Everything is channeled through her. She is the lens your reader looks through when reading your story. Readers want this lens. They covet it." Sacha Black, *10 Steps to Hero: How to Craft Kickass Protagonists*

The hero lens is made up of four parts:
1. Actions
This includes any actions, physical movement, or body language your character does.
2. Thoughts

This includes both inner monologue usually denoted by the use of italics, as well as POV character narration.

3.Dialogue

Does what it says on the tin, anything spoken out loud.

4.Feelings

This includes any emotional showing, telling, visceral reactions and sensations.

But side characters are most definitely not heroes. Thus, what does their lens look like? I call their lens the: **Character Lens.**

The character lens is the lens through which your side character's voice and personality comes to life. Be that through the eyes of a narrator, the protagonist or the characters themselves if they have a POV. It looks a little different to the hero lens as it's broken into two levels:

Character Lens Level 1: action and dialogue

Character Lens Level 2: feelings and thoughts

No matter who is narrating, side characters are in charge of displaying their own actions and dialogue, these are also the story elements that increase immediacy with the reader. To create realistic actions that help deepen characterization, you need to *show* their personality rather than telling it. Feelings and thoughts on the other hand can only be interpreted or inferred by the POV character. Which means they're less immediate and less accurate because they're open to interpretation or misinterpretation.

Emotions drive actions, so if you're ever stuck with how to display a side characters ask yourself:

- What is my character feeling in this moment?
- What is the expected emotional reaction?
- How can I subvert that expectation?
- Can I identify five different actions my character would take based on their current emotion?

Let's look at this in practice. First up, we're going to walk through a protagonist narrating a scene:

The track swept through the middle of the forest in an endless curve toward the horizon. Rows and rows of wooden teeth jutted out from under the tracks like six-year-old nightmares. Wind howled like wolves through the trees, I pulled my jacket tighter, gripping my phone deep in my pocket, praying I still had signal.

Let's go through line by line and explore how this demonstrates each element of the character lens.

The track swept through the middle of the forest in an endless curve toward the horizon. [*this is scene setting and the only hint of personality comes from the word endless which indicates some emotional hesitation towards the track and the forest—let's call it subtext shall we!*] Rows and rows of wooden teeth jutted out from under the tracks like six-year-old nightmares. [*This is the first indication of characterization, rather than describing the wood or the color or perhaps the shape as something harmless, the character is describing the tracks like a nightmare. This augments that first hint of subtext in the previous sentence. This also shows the reader that the character is probably a bit of a wimp and feeling scared rather than being brave or nonplussed*] Wind howled like wolves through the trees, [*sensory description and also another reference to a "monster" showing the character's narrative thoughts are about monsters rather than admiring the scenery*] I pulled my jacket tighter, gripping my phone deep in my pocket, [*this action shows the character's feeling scared and reaching for security/comfort.*] praying I still had signal. [*Another action indicative of the character's state of mind*].

We don't see dialogue but we will in the next snippet that follows on from the above scene.

Non-POV side character:

Okay, now we're going to insert a non-POV side character. Let's examine how this affects the narration and tension and how we can show characterization even when we don't have that specific character as a hero lens.

Jackson bounced out of the woods and onto the track his eyes glittering as he slipped onto the sleepers.

"Get off the track, Jackson, what if a train comes?"

"Chill out. This is amazing." Jumping between the two metallic tracks, his face was bright and wide even in the dimming light.

Once again, let's go through this paragraph and demonstrate how we're using the character and hero lenses to create characterizations and show character.

Jackson bounced out of the woods [*this is the protagonist narrating but Jackson's action of bouncing shows a stark contrast to the narrator's fearful movements*] and onto the track his eyes glittering as he slipped onto the sleepers. [*again, while narrated by the protagonist, his actions show that he is feeling excited and is in a non-fearful mood, glittering eyes suggest mischief as opposed to fear*].

"Get off the track, Jackson, what if a train comes?" I said. [*It's the first bit of dialogue from the protagonist, but it instantly mimics the feelings we've seen in the previous paragraph, ever fearful, this time for Jackson*].

"Chill out. This is amazing," he said [*a clear difference in tone and word choice, his dialogue reflecting how he feels. Chill out indicates that Jackson thinks the protagonist is over reacting.*] jumping between the two metallic tracks. His face was bright and wide even in the dimming light. [*This final line shows both how Jackson is feeling—through his body language—and the protagonist's fear of their current situation. Specifically the "dimming light" is subtext for all the monsters that come out at night. So the protagonist's narration serves doubly here as a character reveal for both of them*].

Now it's your turn.

Take your favorite book in your genre, open to a random scene (that includes multiple characters). Re-read that scene and use the space below to pick out the sentences, or elements of sentences that evoke their character the most.

·

·

·

·

·

·

·

·

Reflect on the above sentences, are there any patterns? What do they tell or show you about the characters? Has the author used any literary tools or devices to create the characterization effect?

·

·

·

·

I want you to write a paragraph from the point of view of your protagonist. If you need a prompt, use this: your protagonist walks into an antique shop and looks around. Then they stumble across a strange object that shouldn't be there.

·

·

-

-

-

-

-

-

Now rewrite the same paragraph inserting one of your major side characters, ensure you use both levels of the character lens to display characterization.

-

-

-

-

-

-

-

Now rewrite the paragraph again and insert a different major side character, still ensuring you use both levels of the character lens to display characterization.

.

.

.

.

.

.

.

.

Okay, we're going to dig deeper this time. Focusing on your major side characters, note down a few of their most salient traits or personality aspects:

Side Character 1:

.

.

.

.

Side Character 2:

.

.

.

.

Side Character 3:

.

.

.

.

Side Character 4:

.

.

.

.

Side Character 5:

.

.

.

.

Now, taking each character in turn and focusing on showing those traits through action and dialogue, write a short scene (use the following prompt for each of those side characters if you need it). Focus on displaying their most salient traits through action and dialogue.

Prompt: your protagonist has fallen in love and your side character doesn't approve.

-
-
-
-
-
-
-
-
-
-

For one of your side characters, include one of the techniques your favorite author used above.

Side Character 1:

-
-

-

-

-

-

-

-

-

-

-

Side Character 2:

-

-

-

-

-

-

-

-

-

-

-

-

Side Character 3:

-

-

-

-

-

-

-

-

-

-

-

Side Character 4:

-

-

-

-

-

-

-

-

-

-

-

Side Character 5:

-

-

-

-

.

.

.

.

.

.

.

.

Subtext

If "text" is the blood-stained ink you scrawl on the page, aka the physical words your reader sees, then subtext is everything else. Everything you haven't said but your reader infers anyway. Subtext is the meaning between the lines. It's the message your readers take from a scene without you explicitly telling them.

You know when you're disagreeing and your partner says, "I'm fine" and yet you know they are anything *but* fine! That is a glorious shining example of subtext.

Subtext helps you show aspects of character and story that you don't want to slap your reader around the face with. You can use subtext to let the reader infer what a non-POV character might be thinking or feeling through descriptions of body language, what's not said, choreography and narrating character's interpretations. One of the best ways to create subtext is by showing your reader what your character is focused on.

So taking the paragraphs you wrote in the last exercise, I want you to edit two of them to include two different types of subtext.

Paragraph 1:

-
-
-
-
-
-
-

Paragraph 2:

-
-
-
-
-
-
-

Quirks

Another tool in your box for deepening characterization for a non-POV side character is to ensure they have a quirk.

"A quirk is unique and idiosyncratic to your character; it's a deliberate behavior. Usually, it will stick out to your reader or other characters. For example, in the movie *East is East*, one character, a young boy called Sajid, refuses to take his jacket off, EVER. He wears it rain, snow, sun or sleeping." Sacha Black, ***10 Steps to Hero: How to Craft a Kickass Protagonist.***

There are two aspects you need to create believable quirks:

- The first is to ensure the quirk has a function in your story
- The second is to show rather than tell the quirk

Thinking about your favorite books in the genre you write in (or your favorite genre-based TV shows and movies), note down a quirk from five different side characters and one way the author has shown the quirk to the reader.

Side Character 1:

.

.

.

.

Shown how?

.

.

.

.

Side Character 2:

-
-
-
-

Shown how?

-
-
-
-

Side Character 3:

-
-
-
-

Shown how?

-
-

-

-

Side Character 4:

-

-

-

-

Shown how?

-

-

-

-

Side Character 5:

-

-

-

-

Shown how?

•

•

•

•

In the spaces below, I want you to note down your side character's quirk and then write a short paragraph where they display their quirk in action:

Side Character 1 Quirk:

•

•

•

•

Quirk in Action:

•

•

•

•

•

•

•

Side Character 2 Quirk:

Quirk in Action:

Side Character 3 Quirk:

·

·

Quirk in Action:

·

·

·

·

·

·

·

·

Side Character 4 Quirk:

·

·

·

·

Quirk in Action:

·

.

.

.

.

.

.

.

Side Character 5 Quirk:

.

.

.

.

Quirk in Action:

.

.

.

.

.

.

.

.

Dialogue

One of the most influential quotes I've ever seen about dialogue is this:

> "Dialogue is communication between characters, not communication between the writer and reader. Do not confuse the two." Gabriela Pereira, *DIY MFA: Write with Focus, Read with Purpose, Build your Community*.

Which means we need to let their voices shine and eradicate "monomouth" a term coined by J. Thorn meaning that all your characters sound the same. We're going to eradicate that now. In discussion with Jeff Elkins, aka The Dialogue Doctor, he told me this:

> "The key to writing long-lasting side characters is strategically creating voices that will complement and contrast with your protagonist's voice, so that your long-lasting side characters will naturally encourage your protagonist and challenge your protagonist toward change and maturity."

He continued to explain that for minor characters, you should aim to make their voices opposite to your protagonist's because they're only brief encounters and therefore the stark contrast sharpens the characterization for both characters.

Another trick for determining your side character's voice is to consider their background. How does it impact their word choice, tone and accent?

Thinking about your favorite books in the genre you write in (or your favorite genre-based TV shows and movies), describe the dialogue for five side characters. Do they have an accent? Do they use slang words? Are they wordy or speak with brevity?

Side Character 1:

·

·

·

·

Side Character 2:

·

·

·

·

Side Character 3:

·

·

·

·

Side Character 4:

.

.

.

.

Side Character 5:

.

.

.

.

Let's dive into some exercises to unearth your character's voices.
Side Character 1:
What common words do they use?

.

.

.

.

Do they use slang? If yes, note it below.

.

.

·

·

What's their background both locationally and professionally and how does this impact the words they use? Note some of the words below.

·

·

·

·

Do they use long sentences or short ones? Write two sentences below in their voice, one where they're telling someone off and one where they're paying a compliment.

·

·

·

·

Do they use commas in excess? Or choppy periods?

·

·

·

·

.

How would you describe the tone of their voice?

.

.

.

.

Now write a conversation between this character and your protagonist about one of your plot problems:

.

.

.

.

.

.

.

.

.

.

·

·

·

·

Side Character 2:
What common words do they use?

·

·

·

·

Do they use slang? If yes, note it below.

·

·

·

·

What's their background both locationally and professionally and how does this impact the words they use? Note some of the words below.

·

·

·

·

Do they use long sentences or short ones? Write two sentences below in their voice one where they're telling someone off and one where they're paying a compliment.

·

·

·

·

Do they use commas in excess? Or choppy periods?

·

·

·

·

How would you describe the tone of their voice?

·

·

·

.

What letter do you associate with the sound of their voice?

.

.

.

.

Now write a conversation between this character and your protagonist about one of your plot problems:

.

.

.

.

.

.

.

.

.

.

.

.

.

.

.

.

.

Side Character 3:
What common words do they use?

.

.

.

.

Do they use slang? If yes, note it below.

.

.

.

.

What's their background both locationally and professionally and how does this impact the words they use? Note some of the words below.

.

.

.

.

Do they use long sentences or short ones? Write two sentences below in their voice one where they're telling someone off and one where they're paying a compliment.

.

.

.

.

Do they use commas in excess? Or choppy periods?

.

.

.

.

How would you describe the tone of their voice?

.

.

.

.

What letter do you associate with the sound of their voice?

.

.

.

.

Now write a conversation between this character and your protagonist about one of your plot problems:

.

.

.

.

.

.

.

.

.

.

.

.

.

.

.

.

Side Character 4:
What common words do they use?

.

.

.

.

Do they use slang? If yes, note it below.

.

.

.

.

What's their background both locationally and professionally and how does this impact the words they use? Note some of the words below.

.

.

.

.

Do they use long sentences or short ones? Write two sentences below in their voice one where they're telling someone off and one where they're paying a compliment.

.

.

.

.

Do they use commas in excess? Or choppy periods?

.

.

.

.

How would you describe the tone of their voice?

.

.

.

.

What letter do you associate with the sound of their voice?

.

.

.

.

Now write a conversation between this character and your protagonist about one of your plot problems:

.

.

.

.

.

.

.

.

.

.

.

.

.

.

.

.

Side Character 5:
What common words do they use?

.

.

.

.

Do they use slang? If yes, note it below.

.

.

.

.

What's their background both locationally and professionally and how does this impact the words they use? Note some of the words below.

.

.

.

.

Do they use long sentences or short ones? Write two sentences below in their voice one where they're telling someone off and one where they're paying a compliment.

.

.

.

.

Do they use commas in excess? Or choppy periods?

.

.

.

.

How would you describe the tone of their voice?

.

.

.

.

What letter do you associate with the sound of their voice?

.

.

.

.

Now write a conversation between this character and your protagonist about one of your plot problems:

.

.

.

.

.

.

.

.

.

.

-

-

-

-

-

STEP 5 WHAT DO SIDE CHARACTERS DO ANYWAY?

In terms of story structure, side characters provide pillars of support to the protagonist. They are neither who the story is about nor the hero of the story. But they do provide either support or hinderance for your protagonist.

Side characters do many things like:

- Work as literary tools / plot devices
- Function as information revealers in the plot
- Provide alternative representations of the theme
- Set the tone for a scene and help to world build
- Create conflict and drive the plot and pace by pushing or pulling the protagonist in different directions
- Narrate or help the author avoid exposition by presenting in a narrator type form which helps the writer to show events rather than telling them

Thinking about your favorite books in the genre you write in (or your favorite genre-based TV shows and movies), note down your 10 favorite side characters and their function in the story.

Character 1:

-

-

-

Function:

-

-

-

Character 2:

-

-

-

Function:

-

-

-

Character 3:

-

-

.

Function:

.

.

.

Character 4:

.

.

.

Function:

.

.

.

Character 5:

.

.

.

Function:

-

-

-

Character 6:

-

-

-

Function:

-

-

-

Character 7:

-

-

-

Function:

-

-

.

Character 8:

.

.

.

Function:

.

.

.

Character 9:

.

.

.

Function:

.

.

.

Character 10:

.

.

.

Function:

.

.

.

Now think about your five main side characters, what is their function in the story?

Side Character 1 Function:

.

.

.

Side Character 2 Function:

.

.

.

Side Character 3 Function:

.

.

.

Side Character 4 Function:

.

.

.

Side Character 5 Function:

.

.

.

Major Story Archetypes

Archetypes are masks worn by characters to serve a particular function at a particular time to move the plot forward. In other words, they're a literary device. Which happens to be what side characters are and unsurprisingly why you find archetypes in side characters. I know, shocking isn't it! The most common mistake writers make with archetypes is assuming that if you pop an archetypal hat on a character that they must stay that way forevermore. Not so, while yes, it does help with character consistency and that helps with characterization and depth, it's not like your virginity—you can take an archetype back!

Major archetypes include:

- The Friend
- The Guide

- The Obstacle
- Hermes
- Sly Fox
- The Joker

Friends provide motivation, conflict, conscience, and companionship. Friends tend to be major side characters with arcs and a lot of page time. Don't make the mistake of thinking they need to be similar to the hero, they don't.

The guide always makes me think of a slew of old beardy wizards! The guide and mentor's primary purpose is to: teach the hero, protect the hero or bestow gifts on them. Guides can be positive or negative.

Obstacles are the testers of your hero, has he leveled up yet? Good, you may move on. While these guys are there to test the hero, they're unlikely to be the actual villain. Try to make your obstacles about the theme and your heroes flaw.

Hermes functions are the harbingers of information, messages, omens, prophecies and more. Some messages are positive, others negative and don't assume it has to be embodied in a character, message functions are letters and owls and invitations too!

Sly Foxes are insidious little nasties, created to make the protagonist doubt the very fiber of their being. These chaps tend to be found earlier in the book, and they can represent as positive or negative characters. One thing you must always do with a sly fox is reveal their true nature and any underhand activities they've been involved with.

Jokers are the fun in any story. Their job is to lighten the mood, bring a smile to the reader and to the other characters, but don't forget, that often, under humor is a layer of truth or meaning which can draw the protagonist's attention to areas they need to work on. These chaps are often—but not always—flat characters without arcs in order to keep their humorous side, they stay as they are.

Side Character Archetypes

Identify which characters in your story fall under the following archetypes, remember you can have more than one and characters can perform more than one role, although it's virtually impossible for them to do more than one simultaneously, so focus on their biggest role.

The Friend

It's unusual for a protagonist not to have a best friend, or if not "best friend" specifically, then a character who is close to them. That's what these characters are. "Friends" are often different to the hero in some way be it moralistically, physically, background etc. These differences help to deepen characterization between both the hero and the friend. In terms of personality, morals, values, dialogue, etc., how is your friend different to your hero?

Usually the Friend function will do one of two things.

- Express the moral behavior the hero should have but can't because he hasn't completed his arc yet—thus guilting the hero into a realization or action.
- Or, on the flip side, expressing the exact opposite moral behavior thus forcing the hero into action to stop them.

Harry Potter—the greedy fuck—has approximately eight bazillion friends, Ron, Hermione, Hagrid, Neville, Luna, the list really is endless. In *Lord of the Rings*, Samwise is Frodo's BFF, *Game of Thrones'* Jon Snow has Ghost the dog, Thelma and Louise, Pooh and Piglet, and Mowgli and Baloo from *The Jungle Book* by Rudyard Kipling. Perhaps one of the more heart breaking friendships I've ever read comes from *Of Mice and Men*, and of course I'm referencing George and Lennie.

Thinking about your genre, favorite books, or TV and movies, identify five characters that play the friend role:

1.

2.

3.

4.

5.

How do these side characters impact the protagonist in their stories? Do they push the hero to change, do they encourage them down a negative path? Are they a moral compass? A shoulder to cry on etc.

1.

2.

3.

4.

5.

Now thinking about your own novel, which of your characters is the Friend function?

.

.

.

Which one of the two functions mentioned above does your side character do?

.

.

.

Write a short scene showing how they embody this behavior in your story and how they present the challenge to your protagonist:

.

.

.

.

.

.

.

.

.

.

.

The Guide

In *10 Steps to Hero: How to Craft a Kickass Protagonist*, I outline the role of the guide.

"The primary purpose of the guide in a story is threefold: **Teach the hero**, whether that's new skills, new knowledge or otherwise. **Protect the hero** from the villain's devilish party tricks. **Bestow gifts on the hero**, from magical death-wielding weapons to the anecdote that helps the hero have an epiphany."

There are positive guides and negative guides. The positive guide is your bog standard mentor, the Dumbledores and Gandalfs of the world, always out for the best interests of the hero and here to help him on his merry way.

The negative guide, though, is not so much here for the hero's good but to drag them into debauchery and chaos—sounds like my kind of fun. Theses mentors know all the naughty tricks in the book and instead of encouraging the hero down the path to heroism, they spend a chunk of time manipulating the hero and leading them toward darkness, villainy and morally unacceptable behaviors.

Positive guide examples include: Alfred Pennyworth is Batman's guide, Giles from *Buffy The Vampire Slayer*, *Dumbledore* from Harry Potter, Gandalf from *Lord of the Rings*, Merlin from King Arthur, Haymitch from *The Hunger Games*, the Fairy Godmother from *Cinderella*, Tyrion Lannister from *Game of Thrones*, and Sebastian the lobster from *The Little Mermaid*.

Negative guide examples include: Littlefinger (Lord Petyr Baelish) in *A Song of Ice and Fire*, John Milton in *The Devil's Advocate*, Alonzo in *Training Day*, Gordon Gekko in *Wall Street* and Tyler Durden from *Fight Club*.

Thinking about your genre, favorite books, or TV and movies, identify five characters that play the guide role:

Guide 1:

Guide 2:

Guide 3:

Guide 4:

Guide 5:

Do these guides teach the hero, protect the hero or bestow gifts on the hero or a mix of all three? Identify what each of the above guides does in their respective stories.

Guide 1:

Guide 2:

Guide 3:

Guide 4:

Guide 5:

Are these guides positive or negative mentors?

Guide 1:

Guide 2:

Guide 3:

Guide 4:

Guide 5:

Now thinking about your own novel, which of your characters is the Guide function?

.

.

.

And what role do they play in terms of teaching, protecting or gifting?

.

.

.

Are they a positive or negative mentor?

.

.

.

Even if your guide doesn't do all three "protect, teach and gift" actions, I want you to write a scene displaying those actions. Write a scene where the guide protects the hero:

.

.

.

.

.

-

-

-

-

-

-

Now rewrite the scene and change the type of protection the guide is giving. For example, if they were protecting the hero physically, now have them protect them mentally or emotionally.

-

-

-

-

-

-

-

-

-

-

.

.

Write a scene where the guide gifts the hero something:

.

.

.

.

.

.

.

.

.

.

.

.

Write a scene where the guide teaches the hero something:

.

.

-
-
-
-
-
-
-
-
-

The Obstacle

Embodied in side characters, the obstacle is there to test your hero and to establish whether or not she's worthy enough to move on to the next step. By "worthy" I mean that she's learned enough about herself and her flaw or the lie she believes to overcome an obstacle that tests her other flaw or the theme. And of course, sometimes that learning is a downward journey before she comes up.

Examples of obstacles include: the Oracle in *The Matrix*, Fluffy the dog in *Harry Potter*, Sir Didymus, the half-fox, half-terrier guard of the bridge in the movie *The Labyrinth*, Saruman from *Lord of the Rings*, The Winter Soldier in *Captain America*, Roz from *Monsters inc.*

Thinking about your genre, favorite books, or TV and movies, identify five characters that play the obstacle role (above examples not allowed):

Obstacle 1:

Obstacle 2:

Obstacle 3:

Obstacle 4:

Obstacle 5:

How do these obstacles test the hero?

Obstacle 1:

Obstacle 2:

Obstacle 3:

Obstacle 4:

Obstacle 5:

And what is the change or outcome of the test?

Obstacle 1:

Obstacle 2:

Obstacle 3:

Obstacle 4:

Obstacle 5:

Thinking about your own book, identify which character plays the obstacle role:

.

.

.

How does this character test the hero?

.

.

.

.

And what is the change or outcome of the test?

.

.

.

Write a scene where your protagonist is tested by one of your obstacle characters using the space below.

.

.

.

Hermes

A Hermes function is the act of bringing and delivering a

message. But this isn't any old message. It's a message with such power it results in action and change. Often, the messages a Hermes function brings are connected to a plot point, the call to action for the hero or some kind of devastating plot twist.

The messages fall into three categories:

- **Good news,** i.e. help is coming—the Harry Potter Owls
- **Bad news,** i.e. winter is coming—*Game of Thrones* motif
- **Prophecies,** i.e. Percy Jackson from *Percy Jackson and The Lightening Thief*. His prophecy says that the next half-blood child of three specific Gods to reach the age of sixteen will make a decision that will either save or destroy Olympus.

Examples of Hermes characters include: the Oracle from the *Matrix* film, she is both guide, obstacle and Hermes. Professor Trelawny from *Harry Potter*, Effie in *The Hunger Games*.

Thinking about your genre, favorite books, or TV and movies, identify five characters that play the Hermes role:

Hermes 1:

Hermes 2:

Hermes 3:

Hermes 4:

Hermes 5:

Now, what is the message and what kind of message do they bring? Positive, negative, prophecy or otherwise?
Hermes 1:
Message:

-

-

-

Positive/Negative/Prophecy:

-

-

Hermes 2:
Message:

-

-

-

Positive/Negative/Prophecy:

-

-

Hermes 3:
Message:

-

-

-

Positive/Negative/Prophecy:

.

.

Hermes 4:
Message:

.

.

.

Positive/Negative/Prophecy:

.

.

Hermes 5:
Message:

.

.

.

Positive/Negative/Prophecy:

.

.

Thinking about your own book, if you have one, identify the character that plays the Hermes function.

.

.

What is their message:

.

.

.

.

Is it positive, negative or a prophecy?

.

.

Write a scene where your Hermes delivers the message to your protagonist:

.

.

.

.

.

-

-

-

-

-

-

-

Now rewrite this scene and flip the message. If it was positive, make it negative, if it was negative make it positive. Focus on how this changes the emotion and relationship tension in your piece.

-

-

-

-

-

-

-

-

.

.

.

Sly Fox

You ever have one of those friends who makes you doubt your very existence? You show them a new outfit and they intentionally hesitate for the briefest of seconds. It's just perceptible enough the doubt seeps into your subconscious and you decide not to wear the outfit after all. Maybe they're more blatant with their disapproval, perhaps they say "mmm nice" instead of "oh my god babe, that's fucking gorgeous". There's something so malicious about indifference, it really is the killer of confidence.

That's what these functions do. Sometimes you need to knock the hero off their perch. Inserting a sly fox can do that.

The main purpose of a sly fox is to insert doubt into both the plot, the reader and the hero's psyche.

A **positive** sly fox will still appear to cast doubt early in the book but, by the end, they are allies, anti-heroes, lovers or other 'good' characters.

This is most common in romance stories where the love interest is often a sly fox.

A **negative** sly fox casts doubt early on like the positive sly fox. But, that's where the similarity ends. These chaps turn out to have ulterior motives, dark sides and/or are out to attack the hero.

Examples of sly foxes include: Keyser Soze from *The Usual Suspects*, who appears as a disabled gentleman throughout the entire film until the end, where his true nature as the perpetrator is revealed. Nikolai Lantsov from Leigh Bardugo's *Grisha* series appears for the first half of *Siege and Storm* (book 2 in the series) as one character, but his true nature as a prince isn't revealed until a crucial point in the book.

Other examples of sly foxes include Scar from *The Lion King*, who makes Simba believe his dad's death was his fault; Dr. Elsa Schneider from *Indiana Jones* and Prince Hans from the Disney movie *Frozen*.

Thinking about your genre, favorite books, or TV and movies, identify five characters that play the Sly Fox role:

Sly Fox 1:

Sly Fox 2:

Sly Fox 3:

Sly Fox 4:

Sly Fox 5:

Are these sly foxes positive or negative?

Sly Fox 1:

Sly Fox 2:

Sly Fox 3:

Sly Fox 4:

Sly Fox 5:

How does each sly fox insert doubt into the story?

Sly Fox 1:

Sly Fox 2:

Sly Fox 3:

Sly Fox 4:

Sly Fox 5:

How is each sly fox's true nature revealed in those stories?

Sly Fox 1:

Sly Fox 2:

Sly Fox 3:

Sly Fox 4:

Sly Fox 5:

Thinking about your own story, which character plays the sly fox?

.

.

.

Are they a positive or negative sly fox?

.

.

.

.

How does your character insert doubt into the story?

·

·

·

·

How is your sly fox's true nature revealed?

·

·

·

·

Write a scene where your sly fox character makes the protagonist doubt themselves:

·

·

·

·

·

·

·

.

.

.

.

Now I want you to rewrite that scene and flip the doubt, if you sly fox was positive make them negative and vice versa. Concentrate on the emotional tension in the scene, how does flipping the positivity of the character's function change the relationship and atmosphere between the two characters?

.

.

.

.

.

.

.

.

.

.

.

.

.

.

.

The Joker

This function is a mood lightener. Which is why it doesn't always have to be embodied in a character, but can be a thing, an event or any other delicious little bite of comedy you can concoct. You know how every friendship group has one diva? The guy or gal whose cutting banter is so on point it makes you drool as they slice down egos and bitch slap dickheads? Those guys are the joker. They're mischievous, playful and bring a bit of fun to the story.

In symbolic terms, the joker represents the need for change. The slapping of characters via banter is a subtle nudge to "sort your shit out".

While these characters revel in the banter, there's often something meaningful behind the quippy wit. Their wit can call attention to hypocrisy, deceptions and dishonesty.

Examples of jokers include: Timon and Pumba from *The Lion King*, Loki from both the mythology and the Marvel movies. Dobby the house elf from *Harry Potter*, The Grinch, The Cat in The Hat, Merry and Pippin from *Lord of The Rings*, Odin and Loki from *American Gods* and The Artful Dodger from *Oliver Twist*, Olaf from *Frozen*, Donkey from *Shrek*.

Thinking about your genre, favorite books, or TV and movies, identify five characters that play the joker role:

Joker 1:

Joker 2:

Joker 3:

Joker 4:

Joker 5:

What change or "wrongness" do these joker characters draw attention to in the hero?

Joker 1:

Joker 2:

Joker 3:

Joker 4:

Joker 5:

This might feel like hoarding, but use the space below to capture your favorite witty line (or two) of theirs.

Joker 1:

Joker 2:

Joker 3:

Joker 4:

Joker 5:

Reflect on the dialogue or lines above. Are there any similarities or patterns to the humor? Can you spot a preference you might have been harboring?

.

.

.

.

.

.

Pick one of the witty scenes you took the dialogue from above, using the same situation—but different dialogue and narration—rewrite the scene using your own joker characters (or make up new joker characters if you don't have any).

.

.

.

.

.

.

.

.

.

.

.

Moving on to your own book, identify which of your characters plays the joker in the space below.

.

.

.

What change or "wrongness" does your joker character draw attention to in the hero?

.

.

.

The World as a Character

This might surprise you, but the world—as in your story world —can also be used as a side character. It's an interesting, if a little unexpected choice for character creation because of course, it's not embodied in a person—under most circumstances. Good world-building adds layers to your story and creates another emotional layer for your readers to connect with. The Capitol from *The Hunger Games* is a disembodied character. Though it's also embodied in President Snow. Hogwarts from *Harry Potter,* is a character because it's staircases move, it's paintings talk, the school is alive.

Identify five different worlds that have distinct personalities from your favorite genre, books, TV or movies:

World 1:

World 2:

World 3:

World 4:

World 5:

Now note down how the author or show makers characterize or personify the world. What is the world's personality?

World 1:

World 2:

World 3:

World 4:

World 5:

How do the above worlds change? Do they have any physical changes? Do they improve or decline? Or stay static?

World 1:

World 2:

World 3:

World 4:

World 5:

Are there any key events or moments that happened in the world's past that impact how the world is today?

World 1:

World 2:

World 3:

World 4:

World 5:

Now thinking about your world, describe your world's personality in two sentences:

.

.

.

.

.

Identify and describe your key story locations:

.

.

.

·

·

Do any of those locations repeat, i.e. do your characters inhabit those locations multiple times? If yes, order them from most frequent to least frequent below:

·

·

·

·

·

·

·

·

·

What are the main characteristics of your setting?

·

·

·

·

·

Which of these characteristics create conflict or support a plot point?

·

·

·

·

·

How does the world push back against the main character's wants and needs?

·

·

·

·

·

How is your protagonist at odds with the world?

·

·

·

·

·

How are your other side characters at odds with the world?

·

·

·

·

·

How has the world shaped the protagonist?

·

·

·

·

·

How has the world shaped your side characters?

·

·

·

·

·

What are the most significant events in your world's history that have helped shape the place it is today?

·

·

·

·

·

Use the space below to create a word list of all the words and synonyms you can think of to create the atmosphere you're after for your world.

·

·

·

·

·

·

-

-

-

-

-

-

-

-

-

-

-

-

STEP 6 ARC WEAVING

Generally speaking, there are three main types of arc: positive, negative and flat.

A positive arc is the most common type of character arc in both genre fiction and film. Especially for protagonists. When talking about the protagonist, they'll begin with some major flaw or personality foible that stops them from growing and developing and defeating the villain. When referring to major side characters, the same principles apply.

A negative arc is the opposite of a positive character arc. If we're talking heroes then they will end the novel in a worse position than they started. Likewise for side characters. As villains are often classed as side characters, this is the most common form of arc for a villain. If a villain were to have a positive arc, this would be called a "redemption arc". One of the more recent examples I've seen of this is Regina the Evil Queen in the TV show *Once Upon a Time*.

A flat arc means your protagonist or side character starts your novel more or less fully formed. In this instance, your story is less about the change your protagonist undergoes and more about the change they invoke in the story or world. For side characters then, the case is also true. Often there is a side character who embodies a positive representation (or sometimes negative) of the theme and remains steadfast to that representation. Think of the BFF who is a good friend throughout the plot.

How to Create a Side Character Arc

The basic requirements for any character arc are:

- Needing or wanting something
- Not being able to get said thing
- Changing or doing something in order to…
- Get the thing!

The difference then, is that we—the reader—may only see points one and four of a side character arc: the want and getting it. Points two and three may be eluded to, referenced in conversation or via flashback or not at all. Of course, that isn't a rule, with some major side characters you will see all four points albeit in much less detail than a protagonist.

But the easiest way of creating a small arc is to show the beginning and the end only.

A word of caution though: if you present a side character one way at the start of your book and then another way at the end, while it creates the sense of an arc, simply presenting the side character one way and then another, without any explanation or justification, will make some readers feel hard done by. It could also make your characters flat and unrealistic.

How then, do you combat that problem?

It doesn't take much to suggest or imply a change in a character. If a conversation is happening about marriage and getting engaged and previously the character was adamant on never getting married, then your protagonist—and reader—will see the shift in mindset, body language, tone, etc.

How do humans indicate a change of opinion?

- Our voice, tone and words change

- Our posture and subconscious body language changes
- Our mindset shifts
- Our actions change

Thinking about your genre, favorite books, or TV and movies, identify five side characters that have a positive arc, negative arc and a flat arc and how their status differs at the end from the start.

Positive arc 1:

.

.

.

Status change:

.

.

.

Positive arc 2:

.

.

.

Status change:

.

.

.

Positive arc 3:

.

.

.

Status change:

.

.

.

Positive arc 4:

.

.

.

Status change:

.

.

.

Positive arc 5:

·

·

·

Status change:

·

·

·

Negative arc 1:

·

·

·

Status change:

·

·

·

Negative arc 2:

·

·

.

Status change:

.

.

.

Negative arc 3:

.

.

.

Status change:

.

.

.

Negative arc 4:

.

.

.

Status change:

.

.

.

Negative arc 5:

.

.

.

Status change:

.

.

.

Flat arc 1:

.

.

.

Any changes at all?

.

.

·

Flat arc 2:

·

·

·

Any changes at all?

·

·

·

Flat arc 3:

·

·

·

Any changes at all?

·

·

·

Flat arc 4:

-

-

-

Any changes at all?

-

-

-

Flat arc 5:

-

-

-

Any changes at all?

-

-

-

Just like your hero, your side characters should have to work for their goals. Beat them down and make it hard for them to attain their deepest desires. It makes for riveting tension and grips readers to the page.

Pick three of the above characters and note down how each of them gets a metaphorical beating by the plot in their story.

How does the author make it difficult for them to fulfill their story arcs?

Side character 1:

-

-

-

Side character 2:

-

-

-

Side character 3:

-

-

-

Thinking about your five main side characters, note down which type of arc they have as well as what their status is at the start versus the end of your story:

Side character 1:

-

-

-

Status change:

.

.

.

Side character 2:

.

.

.

Status change:

.

.

.

Side character 3:

.

.

.

Status change:

.

- .

- .

Side character 4:

- .

- .

- .

Status change:

- .

- .

- .

Side character 5:

- .

- .

- .

Status change:

- .

- .

- .

Take each of your side characters above and plot out the following:

Side character 1:

How is this character flawed at the beginning? (Or strong if a negative arc)

-

-

-

What is it that makes them change *and why?*

-

-

-

What state do they end up in at the end?

-

-

-

How do you make it difficult for them to change?

-

-

-

Side character 2:

How is this character flawed at the beginning? (Or strong if a negative arc)

·

·

·

What is it that makes them change *and why?*

·

·

·

What state do they end up in at the end?

·

·

·

How do you make it difficult for them to change?

·

·

·

Side character 3:

·

·

·

How is this character flawed at the beginning? (Or strong if a negative arc)

·

·

·

What is it that makes them change *and why?*

·

·

·

What state do they end up in at the end?

·

·

·

How do you make it difficult for them to change?

·

·

.

Side character 4:

.

.

.

How is this character flawed at the beginning? (Or strong if a negative arc)

.

.

.

What is it that makes them change *and why?*

.

.

.

What state do they end up in at the end?

.

.

.

How do you make it difficult for them to change?

.

.

.

Side character 5:

.

.

.

How is this character flawed at the beginning? (Or strong if a negative arc)

.

.

.

What is it that makes them change *and why?*

.

.

.

What state do they end up in at the end?

.

.

.

How do you make it difficult for them to change?

.

.

.

Pick one side character above and write a scene where they demonstrate their moment of change.

.

.

.

.

.

.

.

.

.

.

.

·

·

·

Edit that scene to ensure you've focused on the emotion, including sensory details, physiological reactions and dialogue.

·

·

·

·

·

·

·

·

·

·

·

·

·

Repeat the exercise above by picking another side character from your list and write the scene where they demonstrate their moment of change.

Now I want you to edit that scene to ensure you've focused on the emotion, including sensory details, physiological reactions and dialogue.

.

.

.

.

.

.

.

.

.

.

.

.

.

Let's do this one more time, pick a final major side character from your list and write a scene where they demonstrate their moment of change.

-

-

-

-

-

-

-

-

-

-

-

-

-

Now I want you to edit that scene to ensure you've focused on the emotion, including sensory details, physiological reactions and dialogue.

-

-

-

-

-

-

-

-

-

-

-

-

-

Change, Grow, Fall

Within the positive, negative and flat type of character arcs, there's a secondary, nuanced way to classify an arc and that's: change, growth or fall arcs.

Change Arcs

This is understandably the most common form of arc as changing gives the most stark growth on a hero's flaw. Hermione Granger from the *Harry Potter* series undergoes a change arc from bossy know it all to humble, helpful and altogether less irritating. Her end point is a stark contrast from where she began and thus she "changes".

Growth Arcs

While growth arcs are similar to change arcs because they both provide a change of some kind, the change in a growth arc is less radical. Change arcs are total transformations. Growth arcs are... well, growth! The character's initial personality remains intact, they just become a better, more rounded version of themselves by the end of the story.

What does a growth arc look like? Typically they present in one of a variety of forms:

- Learning something new (like the truth about a lie they believed)
- Changing their perspective
- Having a different role in life, their job, their family, etc.

Jamie Lannister in the *Game of Thrones* series is a great example of this. He grows and learns and becomes mildly better than he was at the start, but ultimately ends up in the same place he started—with his sister-lover.

Fall Arcs

This represents a negative arc. As the name suggests, this is a character who falls or declines. They make bad choices, shit goes bad, and in the end they doom themselves to failure. Most often, the villain. Though of course, heroes have fall arcs as do side characters.

The most common outcome of this type of arc is death. That can be a literal or figurative death. Literal death is obvious, but a figurative death could be the death of a fundamental part of their personality, the death of their morality or something else.

Other outcomes include corruption, insanity, imprisonment, disillusionment or any other devastating incident you can think of.

Something to note about this type of arc in particular is that usually, the character damages themselves as well as those around them.

While this type of arc is most commonly found in the villain, it's not isolated to the villain. Walter White, the protagonist from the TV show *Breaking Bad* is a fantastic example of a protagonist with a fall arc.

Thinking about your genre, favorite books, or TV and movies, identify five side characters that have a change arc:

Change arc 1:

Change arc 2:

Change arc 3:

Change arc 4:

Change arc 5:

Identify how these characters change, how do they start and what state do they end up in?

Change arc 1:

Change arc 2:

Change arc 3:

Change arc 4:

Change arc 5:

Thinking about your genre, favorite books, or TV and movies, identify five side characters that have a growth arc:

Growth arc 1:

Growth arc 2:

Growth arc 3:

Growth arc 4:

Growth arc 5:

For the characters that experience a growth arc, identify how these characters grow. What is it they learn or how does their mindset change?

Growth 1:

Growth 2:

Growth 3:

Growth 4:

Growth 5:

Thinking about your genre, favorite books, or TV and movies, identify five side characters that have a fall arc:

Fall arc 1:

Fall arc 2:

Fall arc 3:

Fall arc 4:

Fall arc 5:

For those characters with a fall arc, what kind of death do they experience?

Death 1:

Death 2:

Death 3:

Death 4:

Death 5:

Now thinking about your own characters, reflect on the above types of arc and identify what type of arc your characters have: change, growth or fall.

Side character 1:

Side character 2:

Side character 3:

Side character 4:

Side character 5:

As above, for each of your side characters, either describe the change, explain the growth or describe the type of death they experience.

Side character 1:

Side character 2:

Side character 3:

Side character 4:

Side character 5:

Write a scene for one of your side characters where you fulfill their arc.

.

.

.

.

.

.

.

.

.

.

.

.

Edit that scene to ensure you've focused on the emotion, including sensory details, physiological reactions and dialogue.

.

.

.

.

.

.

.

.

.

.

.

.

Now edit the scene one more time, but this time (unless you've already done this) change the arc so that the character dies.

.

-

-

-

-

-

-

-

-

-

-

-

What impact did this have on the emotion and tension in the scene?

-

-

-

-

-

STEP 7 KILLING YOUR DARLINGS

Broadly speaking, most writers agree that there are a few types of character death. They range from: emotional death, psychological death, philosophical death, occupational death and the slightly more permanent form... actual fucking death.

I'm going to discuss death in literature in terms of just two types of death: actual death which I call **tangible death** and **intangible death.**

Intangible Death

This kind of death is less physical or permanent and more metaphorical.

Emotional death is a form of intangible death. Often found in romance or contemporary stories. Sometimes we need to let go of an emotional grief or an emotion that's holding us back from growing. In *P.S. I Love You*, the protagonist, Holly, needs to learn to move on from the devastating loss of her husband, the acceptance and pushing through grief is the emotion gut punch.

Occupational death is obvious from the name. Let's say your protagonist is a big banker, like Jordan Belfort (a real banker and also protagonist of the novel and film *The Wolf of Wall Street*). In order to learn his lesson about defrauding and manipulating the stock market, he lost his status and occupation as an investment banker when he was caught by the FBI.

Philosophical, moral or value driven death is a type of death that has far reaching consequences for the protagonist.

You'll often see a death like this in a story with a negative story arc or in contradiction, a villain's redemption arc. A great example of this is Regina—The Evil Queen, from the TV show *Once Upon a Time*. She gives up her evil ways, values and desires in a bid to become a better person, thus her old philosophy dies in order for her to progress through that growth.

Personality or Psychological death is a type of death that impacts who the protagonist or side character is. Now, this one comes with a warning, yes, you can change a character, but remember all we get of the protagonist is what's on the page, so if you change them too much, they will no longer feel like the protagonist that started the story. In instances like this, try to only change one aspect, and keep everything else the same.

Tangible Death

Tangible death is your good ol' stab-stab, very permanent, six-feet-under form of death. Enough said.

Thinking about your genre, favorite books, or TV and movies, identify three side characters that experience each type of death. Then explain what part of them dies. Last, explore what the emotional reaction is for the protagonist and other major side characters.

Tangible Death 1:

-

-

Emotional reactions:

-

-

-

-

Tangible Death 2:

-

-

-

-

Emotional reactions:

-

-

-

-

Tangible Death 3:

·

·

·

·

Emotional reactions:

·

·

·

·

Emotional Death 1:

·

·

·

·

What dies?

·

·

·

.

Emotional reactions:

.   .

.

.

.

Emotional Death 2:

.

.

.

.

What dies?

.

.

.

.

Emotional reactions:

.

-

-

-

Emotional Death 3:

-

-

-

-

What dies?

-

-

-

-

Emotional reactions:

-

-

-

-

Occupational Death 1:

-
-
-
-

What dies?

-
-
-
-

Emotional reactions:

-
-
-
-

Occupational Death 2:

-
-

-

-

What dies?

-

-

-

-

Emotional reactions:

-

-

-

-

Occupational Death 3:

-

-

-

-

What dies?

-

-

-

-

Emotional reactions:

-

-

-

-

Philosophical Death 1:

-

-

-

-

What dies?

-

-

-

Emotional reactions:

-
-
-
-

Philosophical Death 2:

-
-
-
-

What dies?

-
-
-
-

Emotional reactions:

-

-
-
-

Philosophical Death 3:

-
-
-
-

What dies?

-
-
-
-

Emotional reactions:

-
-
-
-

Personality Death 1:

-
-
-
-

What dies?

-
-
-
-

Emotional reactions:

-
-
-
-

Personality Death 2:

-
-

.

.

What dies?

.

.

.

.

Emotional reactions:

.

.

.

.

Personality Death 3:

.

.

.

.

What dies?

·

·

·

·

Emotional reactions:

·

·

·

·

Thinking about your five main side characters, if they experience one, identify the type of death they go through as well as what dies:

Side character 1:

·

·

·

·

Side character 2:

·

·

-

-

Side character 3:

-

-

-

-

Side character 4:

-

-

-

-

Side character 5:

-

-

-

-

What consequence does each side character's death have to your plot, other side characters, the tension, pace or emotion?

Side character 1:

-

-

-

-

Side character 2:

-

-

-

-

Side character 3:

-

-

-

-

Side character 4:

-

-

-

-

Side character 5:

-

-

-

-

Note down the emotional reactions from the protagonist and other side characters in the space below.

-

-

-

-

-

-

-

-

Bad Reasons to Kill Characters

Bad reasons to kill a character include:

- It makes readers cry
- You're doing it for effect
- They're a diverse or marginalized character and there's no justifiable reason
- You're Fridging them*
- They're not staying dead

*If you've never come across the term Fridging, it was coined after a comic—The Green Lantern—where the writers killed off the Green Lantern's partner (Alexandra DeWitt) and stuffed her into a refrigerator. This is bad because the only reason for her death was to make the Green Lantern hate Major Force more than he already did. DeWitt's death didn't solve a problem, it didn't twist the plot, its sole consequence was to heighten one man's hate for another man.

Several good reasons to kill a character:

- It provides motivation from a deep emotional place
- It forces a character into the "dark night" which prompts them to change
- It's just plain realistic
- It augments the theme
- It advances the plot
- It completes a character's arc

Thinking about your genre, favorite books, or TV and movies, identify one side character that dies for each of the above reasons.

Death creates motivation:

.

.

Death prompts dark night:

.

.

Death is realistic:

.

.

Death augments theme:

.

.

Death advances the plot:

.

.

Death completes a character's arc:

.

.

In the space below, if you can, try to identify any characters you can think of from your genre, favorite books, or TV and movies, that die for the bad reasons mentioned above.

It made readers cry and that's it:

.

Done for effect:

·

·

They were a diverse character and there was no justifiable reason:

·

·

They were Fridged:

·

·

They didn't stay dead:

·

·

Now, thinking about your own side characters, for the ones who die, note down the reasons why below:

Side character 1:

·

·

·

Side character 2:

-
-
-
-

Side character 3:

-
-
-
-

Side character 4:

-
-
-

Side character 5:

-

.

.

.

Pre-Plot Deaths

A pre-plot death happens before the "present" time in the book you're reading (or writing). For example, in *The Sky is Everywhere*, Bailey—the protagonist's sister—dies before the story begins. It opens with Lennie, the protagonist, reeling from Bailey's death and trying to learn how to live again without her sister.

Thinking about your genre, favorite books, or TV and movies, identify five side characters that die pre-plot.

Side character 1:

.

.

Side character 2:

.

.

Side character 3:

.

.

Side character 4:

.

.

Side character 5:

.

.

For each of those side characters, note down how they influence the story plot in the protagonist's or side character's "present" time-line. Or, what the consequences were of their death and what were the emotional reactions?

Side character 1:

.

.

.

Consequences:

.

.

.

Emotional reactions:

.

.

.

Side character 2:

-

-

-

Consequences:

-

-

-

Emotional reactions:

-

-

-

Side character 3:

-

-

-

Consequences:

-

-

-

Emotional reactions:

-

-

-

Side character 4:

-

-

-

Consequences:

-

-

-

Emotional reactions:

-

-

-

Side character 5:

-

-

-

Consequences:

-

-

-

Emotional reactions:

-

-

-

If you have a pre-plot death that influences your characters in the present, note it down below. If you don't have one, I want you to make one up. Even if you don't end up using it in your novel, this is about practice and filling your writer toolbox with tools!

Pre-plot death character:

-

-

-

Note down how that character is related to your living characters, how they influenced the timeline or the consequences of their deaths.

.

.

.

Write a scene in the *present* timeline of your story where you reference the pre-plot death and the consequences it had on your characters. Note, this doesn't mean you need to write in the present tense, just in the "present" plot.

.

.

.

.

.

.

.

.

.

.

Edit that scene to ensure you've focused on the emotion, including sensory details, physiological reactions and dialogue.

.

.

.

.

.

.

.

.

.

.

.

.

Off Screen Deaths

Pre-plot deaths happen before or during the story, but don't appear on the page. In other words, the reader (and the protagonist) does not see the stab-stab action or the hollow crackle of a dying breath.

An example of an off-screen death include Tonks, Moody, and

Lupin from the final *Harry Potter* book, all of whom die off-screen during the final battle. In the Pixar film *Coco*, Mamá Coco, Miguel's great-grandma passes away at the end of the film, we don't see her death, just her photo placed with the photos of Miguel's other ancestors.

Thinking about your genre, favorite books, or TV and movies, identify five different side character that die off-screen *during* the "present" time of the story.

Side character 1:

.

.

Side character 2:

.

.

Side character 3:

.

.

Side character 4:

.

.

Side character 5:

.

For each of those side characters, note down how they influenced the story plot or what the consequences were of their death and what the emotional reactions were for the protagonist and other side characters.

Side character 1:

.

.

.

.

Consequences:

.

.

.

.

Emotional reactions:

.

.

.

.

Side character 2:

-
-
-
-

Consequences:

-
-
-
-

Emotional reactions:

-
-
-
-

Side character 3:

-
-

·

·

Consequences:

·

·

·

·

Emotional reactions:

·

·

·

·

Side character 4:

·

·

·

·

Consequences:

-

-

-

-

Emotional reactions:

-

-

-

-

Side character 5:

-

-

-

-

Consequences:

-

-

-

Emotional reactions:

·

·

·

·

Use the space below to explore and think about whether any of your characters could or should die off screen during your story, be sure to note the consequences of any death.

·

·

·

·

·

·

·

If you have an "off-screen" death, write out a scene below where your protagonist and living side characters are told the news. If you don't have an off-screen death in your story, write one in. Your character was either: poisoned, died when their car drove off a cliff, murdered or hung.

- .

- .

- .

- .

- .

- .

- .

- .

- .

- .

- .

- .

- .

- .

Meaningful Deaths

How do you create meaningful character deaths? Well…

"Creating pain in death isn't really about losing the person. Of course, that's horrendous and awful. We all know that pain. But what truly conveys the significance of loss to a reader is the intangible thing a hero can't touch…" Sacha Black, *The Anatomy of Prose: 12 Steps to Sensational Sentences*.

What kind of details can help bring that depth?

- Smells you associate with the character
- A habit or quirk they had
- A location the characters used to visit together
- A specific holiday they went on
- An item of clothing or jewelry they always wore
- Another person who was important to them (and why)
- An object, antique or item they loved
- A flower or decoration they loved
- A particular food or drink they always ate / drank

Thinking about any of the side characters you've already identified that died in your favorite genre, books, TV or movies, I want you to note down why their deaths were meaningful and any details you associated with that death.

Side character 1—reason for meaningful death:

.

.

.

.

Details that helped create meaning:

.

.

.

.

Side character 2—reason for meaningful death:

.

.

.

.

Details that helped create meaning:

.

.

.

.

Side character 3—reason for meaningful death:

.

.

.

Details that helped create meaning:

-
-
-
-

Side character 4—reason for meaningful death:

-
-
-
-

Details that helped create meaning:

-
-
-
-

Side character 5—reason for meaningful death:

-

.

.

.

Details that helped create meaning:

.

.

.

.

Thinking about your own side characters, for any characters that die, note down the reason their death is meaningful and any details you can add to help create that meaning.

Side character 1—reason for meaningful death:

.

.

.

.

Details that helped create meaning:

.

.

.

-

Side character 2—reason for meaningful death:

-

-

-

-

Details that helped create meaning:

-

-

-

-

Side character 3—reason for meaningful death:

-

-

-

-

Details that helped create meaning:

-

-

-

-

Side character 4—reason for meaningful death:

-

-

-

-

Details that helped create meaning:

-

-

-

-

Side character 5—reason for meaningful death:

-

-

-

-

Details that helped create meaning:

-

-

-

-

Write a death scene where you take into account everything we've discussed, you include details and references to past things that make the character's life meaningful. Be sure to focus on the emotion in the scene and showing rather than telling.

-

-

-

-

-

-

-

-

-

-

-

-

-

-

-

STEP 8 FIGHT TO THE DEATH

Conflict is vital for your story. Conflict is the source of change. It's the driving force bubbling between the lines of ink.

Creating conflict is as simple as **A + B = C.** Or in literary terms, **The existence of a goal + prevention of the goal being achieved = conflict.**

Create a goal. Stop the goal coming to fruition. Usually we think of goals in terms of the hero because the hero's goal is driving the plot. But we're here to focus on the side characters.

1. What's your side character's goal?
2. What are you going to do to stop her from getting it?

But before you answer those questions, I want you to think about your five favorite side characters (ideally in the genre you write in). What are their goals, and what barriers does the author put in place to stop them from coming to fruition?

Side character 1 goal:

.

·

·

Side character 2 goal:

·

·

·

Side character 3 goal:

·

·

·

Side character 4 goal:

·

·

·

Side character 5 goal:

·

·

·

Side character 1 barrier:

-

-

-

Side character 2 barrier:

-

-

-

Side character 3 barrier:

-

-

-

Side character 4 barrier:

-

-

-

Side character 5 barrier:

-

.

.

Thinking about your own side characters, what are their goals and what barriers have you put in place to stop them achieving them?

Side character 1 goal:

.

.

.

Side character 2 goal:

.

.

.

Side character 3 goal:

.

.

.

Side character 4 goal:

.

.

Side character 5 goal:

Side character 1 barrier:

Side character 2 barrier:

Side character 3 barrier:

Side character 4 barrier:

-

-

-

Side character 5 barrier:

-

-

-

There are three main types of conflict which I explained in my book *10 Steps to Hero: How to Craft a Kickass Protagonist.*

"**Macro conflict** - These are large scale world wars, society against the hero, often found in dystopian novels as the 'final' villain that needs defeating. But this could be any war that spans more than just the hero. It could cross states, history, natural forces, the law, races and more. For example, the faction system that categorizes every citizen in the *Divergent* series by Veronica Roth, or the man-killing Triffid plants in *The Day of The Triffids* by John Wyndham.

Micro conflict - This is a more interpersonal form of conflict—the battles the hero has with personal relationships, for example, between lovers, friends, family, colleagues and enemies. In *Me Before You* by Jojo Moyes, the entire plot is based on a micro conflict. Will has a motorcycle accident that leaves him with a desire to end his life. Until Lou rolls into his world and tries to change his mind. Their desires: Lou's love for him, and his desire to die, smash into each other as they are in direct opposition.

Inner conflict - This is the smallest unit of conflict as it's internal only to the hero. It's the conflict the hero has with his own flaws, emotions and values. While it's the most isolated conflict, it's usually the most heart-wrenching as it's the conflict closest to the reader—particularly if you write in closer points of view like first person or third person limited. *Game of Thrones* by George R.R. Martin is rife with inner conflict. One of Martin's specialties is giving characters conflicting values and loyalties. Jamie Lannister (known as the Kingslayer) killed the very king he swore to protect."

Thinking about your genre, favorite books, or TV and movies, identify three different types of conflict for macro, micro and inner forms of conflict.

Macro 1:

.

.

.

Macro 2:

.

.

.

Macro 3:

.

.

.

Micro 1:

-

-

-

Micro 2:

-

-

-

Micro 3:

-

-

-

Inner 1:

-

-

-

Inner 2:

-

·

·

Inner 3:

·

·

·

Thinking about your own book, identify as many forms of each type of conflict as you can.

Macro 1:

·

·

·

Macro 2:

·

·

·

Macro 3:

·

·

·

    Micro 1:

·

·

·

    Micro 2:

·

·

·

    Micro 3:

·

·

·

    Inner 1:

·

·

·

    Inner 2:

.

.

.

Inner 3:

.

.

.

Types of Inner Conflict

Some ideas for generating inner conflict include:

- Love
- Values and Morals
- Beliefs
- Self-image
- Religion
- Politics
- Existential

Can you identify one story from your genre that has inner conflict falling under each one of the above prompts/ideas?

Love:

.

.

Values and Morals:

-

-

Beliefs:

-

-

Self-image:

-

-

Religion:

-

-

Politics:

-

-

Existential:

-

-

Write a scene below using one of the above prompts where one of your side characters is experiencing inner conflict. First, write this scene from the point of view of your side character.

-
-
-
-
-
-
-
-
-
-
-
-

Now rewrite the scene from the point of view of your protagonist.

-

-

-

-

-

-

-

-

-

-

-

-

-

Reflecting on the above exercises: what emotional beats does your protagonist miss that your side character felt when you were in their POV?

-

-

-

Does your protagonist misinterpret anything the side character does?

.

.

.

.

What did you learn about showing emotional conflict from switching between POVs?

.

.

.

.

Micro Conflict

Micro conflict is a step up and out from inner conflict. It's where side characters really come into their own. Micro conflict is a more interpersonal form of conflict—it's the battles characters have with personal relationships, between lovers, friends, family, colleagues and enemies, etc.

One area that does bear repeating are conflict consequences. Consequences are the absolute do or die, must-not-be-forgotten aspect of conflict.

For the first 75% of your novel, the majority of consequences should be negative. This negative consequence will create plot problems and complications which drive the action forward and your protagonist towards the climax of your story.

Let's just throw some consequences out there. Here are a few ideas of consequences:

- Loss of relationship, friendship or lover
- More difficult, longer or complex journey
- Loss of power be it magical, authoritative or intangible
- Loss of or unable to retrieve information
- Loss of or unable to retrieve a needed item
- Loss of confidence, self-belief or other positive self-worth and value like…
- Loss of home, safety or food source

Something to consider when creating your micro conflict is the need to ensure it's realistic. It's no good having two characters flop about on the page like suffocating fish. This shit needs to be deep and intense and meaningful.

But how do you create that level of argumentative intensity?

1. Specificity

Whatever the conflict, it needs to be specific. The more generalized a conflict, the harder it is to hook it to a particular person.

2. Meaning

As well as being specific to each character, micro conflicts need to mean something to the characters.

3. Connect theme to micro conflict

If you want to sprinkle a little pizazz on your micro conflict, you can connect it to the theme. For example, in the movie *G.I. Jane*, most of the conflict in the film was based on sexism and reducing Jane's female power. Master Chief—her trainer, boss, mentor and general thorn in her side—constantly disrespected her, assumed she was weak and pitiful *because* she was a woman. They fought and fought and she had to earn every ounce of respect from him, which in the ultimate girl power move, Master Chief gets shot and she picks his bleeding ass up and carries him out a war zone to safety. She triumphed as a powerful woman and he ended up respecting her for it.

Thinking about your genre, favorite books, or TV and movies, identify five different side characters who experience micro conflict (note, these can be the same as above but if you can think of different ones to last time, do). Identify how each of these types of conflict is specific, meaningful and connects to the theme:

Side character micro 1:

-

-

-

-

How is it specific?

-

-

-

-

How is it meaningful?

-

-

-

-

How does it connect to the theme?

-

-

-

-

Side character micro 2:

-

-

-

-

How is it specific?

-

-

-

-

How is it meaningful?

-

-

·

·

How does it connect to the theme?

·

·

·

·

Side character micro 3:

·

·

·

·

How is it specific?

·

·

·

·

How is it meaningful?

-

-

-

-

How does it connect to the theme?

-

-

-

-

Side character micro 4:

-

-

-

-

How is it specific?

-

-

-

·

How is it meaningful?

·

·

·

·

How does it connect to the theme?

·

·

·

·

Side character micro 5:

·

·

·

·

How is it specific?

·

·

.

.

.

How is it meaningful?

.

.

.

.

How does it connect to the theme?

.

.

.

.

Identify three types of micro conflict from your own book. Include how the conflict is specific, meaningful and how it connects to your book's theme.

Side character micro 1:

.

.

.

.

How is it specific?

.

.

.

.

How is it meaningful?

.

.

.

.

How does it connect to the theme?

.

.

.

.

Side character micro 2:

.

·

·

·

How is it specific?

·

·

·

·

How is it meaningful?

·

·

·

·

How does it connect to the theme?

·

·

·

·

Side character micro 3:

.

.

.

.

How is it specific?

.

.

.

.

How is it meaningful?

.

.

.

.

How does it connect to the theme?

.

.

.

.

Okay, let's look at some specific sources for creating micro conflict.

- Family
- Secrets and Lies—keeping secrets, spilling secrets, etc.
- Competition
- Doubt
- Misunderstandings and Assumptions

Can you identify one story from your genre that has micro conflict falling under each one of the above prompts/ideas?

Family:

.

.

Secrets and Lies:

.

.

Competition:

.

.

Doubt:

.

.

Misunderstandings and Assumptions:

.

.

Write a scene below using one of the above prompts where one of your side characters is experiencing micro conflict. First, write this scene from the point of view of your side character.

.

.

.

.

.

.

.

.

.

.

.

.

.

.

.

Now rewrite the scene from the point of view of your protagonist.

.

.

.

.

.

.

.

.

.

.

.

.

.

.

Reflecting on the above exercises: what emotional beats does your protagonist miss that your side character felt when you were in their POV?

.

.

.

.

Does your protagonist misinterpret anything the side character does?

.

.

.

.

What did you learn about showing emotional conflict from switching between POVs?

.

.

.

.

Macro Conflict

This type of conflict is the hardest to connect to side characters because it's world facing rather than person to person. Macro conflict is a big bad wolf with no face—much like the corporate conglomerate organizations so many of us used to (or still do) work for. You can't ever put your finger on the real villain because the organization itself is intangible and yet so many of them do untold damage. This is the problem with macro conflict.

It's also why it's so important to build solid reasons for your side characters to engage with the macro conflict.

Let's use *The Hunger Games* as an example. The Capitol—the capital city of Katniss's world is the true villain. It stands for incredibly dark morals like segregation, death, control and sacrifice. But there is the connection to the theme. The book's theme is sacrifice, and The Capitol demands that each district in its locale sacrifice two children to its annual televised games: The Hunger Games. The games themselves create micro conflict in the battles between the children, but seeded in the games is the macro conflict that culminates in the final book—Katniss against The Capitol itself. And here is a couple of examples of where the macro conflict is made specific to the characters:

- The most generic connection is that the Capitol have tried to kill and control Katniss through the games and after the games in her new life.
- One step more specific, The Capitol control how much food and the resources her district receive access too. Meaning all the people she loves and cares about are at the whims of The Capitol.
- And now most specifically, Katniss's sister is threatened multiple times, starting with being picked during the Reaping (for the games) and ultimately when she's then killed as a result of The Capitol and the war.

If the macro conflict weren't connected to Katniss on these multiple layers, her sister's death would be less meaningful.

Thinking about your genre, favorite books, or TV and movies, can you identify three additional macro conflicts?

Macro 1:

-
-
-

Macro 2:

-
-
-

Macro 3:

-
-
-

Pick one of the macro conflicts from the three mentioned here and the three at the top of the chapter. In the same way I did with *The Hunger Games,* break down how the macro conflict is specific to the protagonist or the side characters.

-
-

-

-

-

-

-

-

-

If you're including a macro conflict in your own novel, note a description of it in the space below:

-

-

-

-

How does the conflict impact your protagonist and side characters?

-

-

-

-

Why do your side characters and protagonist care about this conflict?

.

.

.

.

How is the macro conflict connected to your theme?

.

.

.

.

How can you represent that connection in an event in your plot?

.

.

.

.

Do you have side characters on both sides of the conflict? If yes, which ones, if no, create some in the space below.

.

·

·

·

What would winning this macro conflict mean for the theme and your characters?

·

·

·

·

Now write a scene from a side characters point of view where they encounter the macro conflict.

·

·

·

·

·

·

·

.

.

.

.

.

.

.

.

Now re-write this scene from your protagonist's point of view.

.

.

.

.

.

.

.

.

·

·

·

·

·

·

What did you learn from changing the POV? How did it change the emotional tension in the scene? How did it change the pace and level of detail you brought to the scene?

·

·

·

·

Side Character Climaxes

Side character climaxes are the moment their story arc is concluded. While your side characters can and probably should play a role in the story climax, it shouldn't be *the* "winning" role. They can't make the final villain-defeating blow. So how can side characters be involved in the climax of your story?

They help, support, pressure or influence your protagonist to move towards the story climax.

On the flip-side they hinder, distract, or pull your protagonist away from the story conclusion. In this instance, your side character is impacted negatively by your story climax and most often, that's a result of the protagonist's choices.

They're not involved in the story climax, but represent it earlier in the book, be that symbolically, in some kind of foreshadowing mechanism or otherwise.

They provide information, knowledge or a key item which helps the protagonist reach their ultimate goal.

Thinking about your genre, favorite books, or TV and movies, can you identify how five of your already identified side characters have their stories concluded?

Side character 1:

.

.

What role do they play in the overall story climax?

.

.

.

.

Side character 2:

.

.

What role do they play in the overall story climax?

.

-
-
-

Side character 3:

-
-

What role do they play in the overall story climax?

-
-
-
-

Side character 4:

-
-

What role do they play in the overall story climax?

-
-
-

Side character 5:

.

.

What role do they play in the overall story climax?

.

.

.

.

Thinking about your own side characters, how does each one have their character arc or subplot concluded? This is a helpful exercise for picking out loose plot threads or unfinished story loops!

Side character 1:

.

.

.

.

What role do they play in the overall story climax?

.

.

-

-

Side character 2:

-

-

-

-

What role do they play in the overall story climax?

-

-

-

-

Side character 3:

-

-

-

-

What role do they play in the overall story climax?

·

·

·

·

Side character 4:

·

·

·

·

What role do they play in the overall story climax?

·

·

·

·

Side character 5:

·

·

·

.

What role do they play in the overall story climax?

.

.

.

.

WANT MORE?

There's just three more things to say before you go:

First of all, you can get your exclusive side characters checklist by signing up to my mailing list by visiting: sachablack. co.uk/Sidecharacters

Secondly, I hope you found this book helpful in your quest to craft better side characters. If you liked the book and can spare a few minutes, I would be really grateful for a short review on the site from which you purchased the book. Reviews are invaluable to an author as it helps us gain visibility and provides the social proof we need to continue selling books.

Third, if you're looking for a supportive writing community, I run a Facebook group where I host a weekly accountability thread, writing prompts, and more. Join us here: facebook.com/ groups/rebelauthors

From me to you, thank you for reading *8 Steps to Side Characters Workbook* and good luck with your writing journey.

ALSO BY SACHA BLACK

The Better Writers Series

Sacha has a range of books for writers. If you want to improve your villains, your heroes or your prose, she's got you covered.

To improve your villains:

13 Steps to Evil: How to Craft a Superbad Villain

13 Steps to Evil: How to Craft a Superbad Villain Workbook

To improve your heroes:

10 Steps to Hero: How to Craft a Kickass Protagonist

10 Steps To Hero - How To Craft A Kickass Protagonist Workbook

To improve your prose:

The Anatomy of Prose: 12 Steps to Sensational Sentences

The Anatomy of Prose: 12 Steps to Sensational Sentences Workbook

The 9 Things Series with J Thorn:

9 Things Career Authors Don't Do: Personal Finance

9 Things Career Authors Don't Do: Rebel Mindset

ABOUT THE AUTHOR

Sacha Black is a bestselling and competition winning author, rebel podcaster, speaker and casual rule breaker. She has five obsessions; words, expensive shoes, conspiracy theories, self-improvement, and breaking the rules. She also has the mind of a perpetual sixteen-year-old, only with slightly less drama and slightly more bills.

Sacha writes books about people with magical powers and other books about the art of writing. She lives in Cambridgeshire, England, with her wife and genius, giant of a son.

When she's not writing, she can be found laughing inappropriately loud, blogging, sniffing musty old books, fangirling film and TV soundtracks, or thinking up new ways to break the rules.

sachablack.co.uk/newsletter

www.sachablack.co.uk
sachablack@sachablack.co.uk

Image Credit @Lastmanphotography

- instagram.com/sachablackauthor
- bookbub.com/authors/sacha-black
- facebook.com/sachablackauthor
- twitter.com/sacha_black
- amazon.com/author/sachablack

Made in the USA
Monee, IL
21 February 2023

28414242R00167